爱我中华

FOR THE LOVE OF CHINA

中国现代版画藏品集

A COLLECTION OF CONTEMPORARY
CHINESE PRINTS

Novel Energy Art Collection

永新能源 艺术收藏

情系中华

For The Love Of China

中国现代版画藏品集

A COLLECTION OF CONTEMPORARY CHINESE PRINTS

目　录

画家与作品 The Artists and

画家排名按字母顺序 the namelist is in alphabetorder

CONTENTS

Their Works

画家与作品The Artists and

画家排名按字母顺序 the namelist is in alphabetorder

Their Works

弘扬民族文化，促进艺术交流

贺中国版画收藏系列出版

王琦

中国版画家协会主席

中央美术学院教授

Enhance national culture, promote exchanges in the arts

Congratulations on the series of publications on the collecting of Chinese prints

Wang Qi

Chair of the Chinese Printmaker's Association

Professor, The Central Academy of Fine Arts

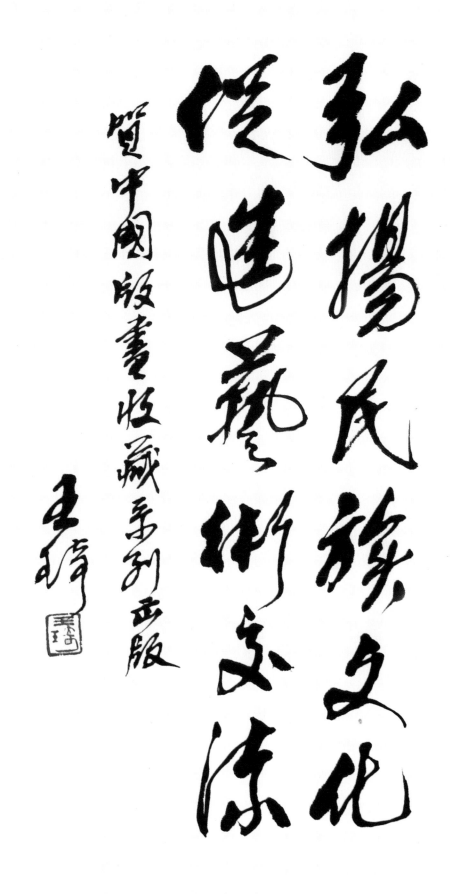

弘扬民族文化
恨哇藝術交流

暨中國版畫收藏系列出版

王琦

王琦　中国版画家协会主席
Wang Qi，Chair of the Chinese Printmaker's Association

赞助人 PATRON

刘钱崧先生
总裁兼首席执行官

刘钱崧先生于 1993 年被任命为哈斯基石油（现哈斯基能源）有限公司的首席执行官。他毕业于澳大利亚昆士兰大学，拥有经济学和商务学双学士学位。刘先生也是澳大利亚会计学会、香港会计学会、香港税务学会以及英国专业管理秘书学会的院士级会员。

刘先生作为总裁和首席执行官，在哈斯基能源的董事会中负责公司的运筹和决策。在加入哈斯基石油公司之前，刘先生曾在长江实业集团（控股）有限公司以及和记黄埔集团有限公司多次担任资深行政要职。

Mr. John C.S. Lau
President & Chief Executive Officer

Mr. John C.S. Lau was appointed Chief Executive Officer of Husky Oil (now Husky Energy) in 1993. He holds a Bachelor of Economics degree and a Bachelor of Commerce degree from the University of Queensland, Australia. Mr. Lau is a Fellow Member of the Institute of Chartered Accountants in Australia, the Australian Society of Accountants, the Hong Kong Society of Accountants, the Taxation Institute of Hong Kong and the Institute of Chartered Secretaries of Administrators of the United Kingdom.

As President & Chief Executive Officer, Mr. Lau is a member of Husky's Board of Directors and is responsible for Husky's corporate direction, strategic planning and corporate policies. Prior to joining Husky, Mr. Lau served in a number of senior executive roles within the Cheung Kong (Holdings) Limited and Hutchison Whampoa Limited group of companies.

刘钱崧

John C.S. Lau

赞助人 PATRON

曹其镛先生

曹其镛先生于 1939 年生于上海。1962 年毕业于日本东京大学，并在 1964 年美国伊利诺州立大学获得硕士文凭。随后在 1965 年加入永新集团任董事。1987 年任职永新企业有限公司总经理，并由 1996 年 7 月至今为董事及副董事长。曹先生现在亦为中国人民政治协商会议浙江省常委。

Mr. Ronald K. Y. Chao

Mr. Chao was born in Shanghai, China in 1939. He was graduated in BS Mechanical Engineering from University of Tokyo in 1962 and received his MSc in Mechanical Engineering from University of Illinois in 1964. Mr. Chao joined Novel as a Director in 1965. He was Managing Director of Novel Enterprises Limited from 1987 and has served as a Director and Vice Chairman since July 1996. He is also a Standing Member of Zhejiang Provincial Committee of the Chinese People's Political Consultative Conference (CPPCC).

曹其镛

Ronald K. Y. Chao

主办人 ORGANIZER

王柏年

王柏年先生自 1986 年起担任加拿大北美永新能源有限公司总裁至今。王柏年先生 1952 年出生于上海，1957 年移民香港，1975 年在内布拉斯加州州立大学（Nebraska）取得机械工程学士学位，同年移民至加拿大。他先后在多家北美跨国公司担任技术和管理职位，例如：福特汽车公司（Ford Motor Canada），柏克德公司（Bechtel Canada），巴杰尔工程公司（Badger USA）和开利空调制冷公司（The Carrier Air Conditioning Corporation）。

王柏年先生在 1984−1986 年期间担任加拿大阿尔伯塔省政府的经济发展部中国局局长（The Director of The Department of Economic Development, Government of Alberta, Canada）。

王柏年先生与阮慧珍女士结婚已有 28 年，膝下子女已经成年，女儿王正如，儿子王佑生。

Pa (Ning) Wong

Pa (Ning) Wong has been the President of Novel Energy (North America) Ltd. since 1986.Born in Shanghai, Pa Wong moved to Hong Kong in 1957. He is a Graduate of The University of Nebraska, Lincoln, Nebraska, with a Degree in Mechanical Engineering.

Mr. Wong immigrated to Canada in 1975. He has held many technical and managerial positions with multinational corporations such as Ford Motor Canada, Bethel Canada, Badger USA and the Carrier Air Conditioning Corporation.

Between 1984 and 1986, Mr. Wong served as the Director of The Department of Economic Development, Government of Alberta, Canada.

Mr. Wong has been married to his wife, Liza Yuen for 28 years, they have two adult children Rachel and Brendan.

Dear Paul,
Lets celebrate the joy
of Art.

Pa Wong
May 10, 2007

王柏年
Pa (Ning) Wong

序　PREFACE

2004年7月，我的儿子——王佑生在哈佛读书时，我们参观了哈佛大学美术馆。在馆藏中，看到了众多文化精品，有许多作品令人怦然心动，但令人遗憾的是其中缺少作为中国传统文化的代表之一的版画精品。

中国版画有1300多年的历史，其内容和形式博大精深。我在国内接触了一些版画作品和作者，这些作品传达的理念，作者的创作精神深深地打动了我，使我爱上了中国版画。去年9月，我向哈佛大学捐赠了林军先生的版画作品—《练兵场的早晨》。从那时起，我们在北京、天津、上海、重庆、广州、深圳、成都、长春、哈尔滨等地陆续收集了国内著名版画家的作品400余幅，在收集整理的过程中，我们还请了上海大学美术学院的刘双先生去这些地方对画家进行了专访，了解画家的创作经历和作品的时代背景，收集了画家资料。

经过近一年的努力，今天《爱我中华—中国现代版画藏品集》终于与中外读者见面了。我们还将采访画家的经过制作成纪录片，从作者的生平和经历着手，就作品的审美特征进行分析说明，以求帮助读者理解作品的全部意义。

我热爱中国文化，并愿意为促进中外文化交流做点有意义的事。为此，我们非常愿意将这些版画作品以及介绍画家的纪录片，无偿提供给各国博物馆、美术馆展出，希望能有更多喜爱中国文化的人对中国版画产生兴趣，让世界更了解中国。

展览活动和版画的结集出版工作得到了国内外热爱中国版画艺术的朋友们的大力支持，在此深表谢意。

王柏年　总裁
永新能源

When Brebdan Wong, my son, was following his summer program in Harvard University in July 2004, He and I paid a visit to Harvard Museum. Among the Museum's collection we saw many marvelous and distinguished art works. But it is regrettable that there are no woodcut works, given that the woodcut is one of the representative element of Chinese traditional culture.

Chinese woodcuts have a history of 1300 years with profound content and expression, I made an opportunity to contact some Chinese woodcut artists and see their works. The concepts they deliver and creative spirit impressed me so much that I came to love Chinese woodcuts. Last year I donated the woodcut 'Morning on the parade ground' by Lin Jun to Harvard University. From then on the Company collected more than 400 woodcuts from artists from Beijing, Tianjin, Shanghai, Chongqing, Guangzhou, Shenzhen, Chendu, Changchun and Haerbin. While collecting these works, we invited Mr. Liu Shuang from the Fine Art College of Shanghai University to go to these cities to interview the artists and to record their creative experiences together with some background information on the works and to gather information about the artists as well.

After one year's hard effort, 'For the love of China – A collection of contemporary Chinese prints' can finally be presented to both The Chinese and overseas public. We have also made a record of the process of the interviews to help readers of the catalogue to fully understand the works with an analysis and explanation of the aesthetic characteristics of the works and to introduce the artists and their experiences.

I love Chinese culture and wish to do something meaningful to help promote the exchange of Chinese culture with foreign countries. Therefore, the Company is willing to offer these woodcuts and the catalogue to museums and art galleries world-wide to exhibit without charge in the hope that more people who love Chinese culture will become interested in Chinese woodcuts and come to know more about China.

We would like to express our sincere gratitude to friends in China and overseas who share our love for Chinese woodcuts and have given great assistance and support to the exhibition and publication of our art collection.

Pa Wong, President
Novel Energy

哈佛大学图书馆收藏

练兵场的早晨　林军
Morning on the parade ground
Lin Jun

哈佛的来信

尊敬的王先生：

我们写这封信来表达我们的感激之情，同时对于您捐给哈佛大学艺术博物馆版画收藏部主任 Marjorie B.Cohn 的林军先生的《练兵场的早晨》，正式的表示感谢，我们很高兴在十月一日收到了这幅木版画。这幅画创作于 1961 年，这个时期正是画家职业生涯从军民题材向更广泛的题材过渡的时期，在画中，人物经常和风景结合在一起。这幅画在一系列战争时期军队题材的画中是很有影响力的一幅，枝繁叶茂的树下，大声讲话的人们暗示着军队里吵闹的声音。

这幅画作为我们永久的收藏，将对我们收藏 20 世纪中国版画具有重要的意义，将提高我们教育、研究、展览的能力。最后，您的礼物对于我们整个美术馆，和下一代学生都是很有帮助的。您的慷慨对于我们全体职员和公众都是受益匪浅的。

附上我们的礼物表，请您填好后寄回，这将作为 2004 年的礼物被记录下来。再一次感谢您对美术馆的慷慨。

Thomas Lentz
哈佛大学美术馆馆长

HARVARD UNIVERSITY ART MUSEUMS

32 Quincy Street
Cambridge, MA 02138
www.artmuseums.harvard.edu

October 8, 2004

Mr. Pa Wong
3947 Edenstone Road, N. W.
Calgary, Alberta
T3A 327
Canada

Dear Mr. Wong,

I am writing to extend both our genuine gratitude and formal thanks for your generous gift of *Morning at the Drill Ground* by Lin Ju to the Harvard University Art Museums. Marjorie B. Cohn, our curator of prints, presented this woodcut at our October 1st acquisitions meeting, and we are delighted to accept it. This print was created in 1961, at a moment in the artist's career when he had passed from the compact figural compositions of troops and civilians to more expansive compositions, where figures are usually integrated into landscapes. This print is one of the most effective of these, with the ranks of troops embodied in the flights of steps, and the cacaphony of martial music implied by the turbulent foliage of the tree in which the loud speaker is hung.

Accepting this work into our permanent collection will contribute significantly to our growing collection of 20th-century Chinese prints, which in turn enhances our teaching, research and exhibition capabilities. Ultimately, your gift advances the mission of this institution, and future generations of students, faculty and the public will enjoy the benefits of your generosity.

I enclose our deed of gift form for you to fill out and return. This will be recorded as a 2004 gift. Once again thank you for your generosity to the Art Museums.

With best wishes,

Thomas W. Lentz
Elizabeth and John Moors Cabot Director

TWL:dd

Cc: Marjorie B. Cohn

尊敬的王先生：

　　昨天当我回到办公室的时候，收到了您寄来的林军的版画作品《长征》，我非常抱歉没有和您和您的家人见面，但是我们 Mongan 中心研究室的主管 Mazie Harris 告诉我，您在这里过得非常愉快，并且她交给我一张 CD。

　　想象一下当我打开 CD 的时候是多么的惊讶，我从来没有收到过一份电子的收藏档案。这真的是非常让人惊讶，CD 里面记录了林军的所有作品，同时它让我意识到了林军在 20 世纪中国艺术界的重要性。我非常感谢您，并不只是因为您的礼物，同样感谢您带给我的这个新的观点。

　　这幅版画本身是一幅非常好的作品，它有着独立的主题，能够拥有这件艺术品我们感到非常骄傲。非常感谢。

　　我的感谢是发自内心的，并不是代表美术馆的官方谢意。我将在九月把版画交给我们的馆长，这是正式接受艺术捐赠所必需的步骤。在见过我们的主任 Thomas Lentz 后，我们将正式的通知您我们收到了捐赠，感谢您为美术馆所作的一切。

　　借此机会，送上我的感谢和最好的祝福。

Marjorie B.Cohn
哈佛大学美术馆版画收藏部主任

FOGG ART MUSEUM

Harvard University Art Museums
32 Quincy Street
Cambridge, MA 02138
www.artmuseums.harvard.edu

25 August 2004

Pa Wong
3947 Edenstone Road, N.W.
Calgary, Alberta
CANADA T3A 327

Dear Pa Wong,

Your gift of the woodcut of the Long March by Lin Ju awaited me on my return to work yesterday. I was so sorry to have missed you and your family, but Mazie Harris, the Mongan Center study room supervisor, told me that your visit was a real pleasure, and she passed along to me the CD.

Imagine my amazement when I opened the CD! I have never before had an electronic dossier for an acquisition. It was marvelous to page through all of the reproductions of Lin Ju's work, and I now understand his great importance in 20th-century Chinese art. I am so grateful to you, not only for your gift but also for your bringing this new perspective to us.

The woodcut itself is a wonderful work. We are honored to have it as a work of art, quite independent of its important subject. Thank you so much.

My thanks are heartfelt, but not the official thanks of the Art Museums. I shall present the woodcut to our curators committee in September, which is necessary for formal acquisition of works of art. After the meeting our director, Thomas Lentz, will write you notifying you of the work's acceptance and thanking you on behalf of the Art Museums.

In the meantime, with my thanks and best wishes,

Sincerely yours,

Marjorie B. Cohn
Carl A. Weyerhaeuser Curator of Prints
Senior Lecturer in History of Art and Architecture

TEL: (617) 495-2393
FAX: (617) 496-3800
E-M: cohn@fas.harvard.edu

ARTHUR M SACKLER MUSEUM   BUSCH-REISINGER MUSEUM   FOGG ART MUSEUM   STRAUS CENTER FOR CONSERVATION

主编 CHIEF EDITOR

齐凤阁

齐凤阁，1974 年毕业于东北师范大学美术系，1982 年毕业于该校中文系，1988 至 1990 年公派日本留学。1992 年晋升为教授，1993 年获国务院政府特殊津贴。曾任东北师范大学美术系主任、美术学硕士研究生导师、吉林省美术家协会副主席。现任深圳大学艺术与设计学院院长、教授，中国美术家协会版画艺委会副主任，《中国版画》杂志主编。被聘为第 8、9、10 届全国美术展览评委，第 14、15、16、17 届全国版画展及北京国际版画展、"今日中国美术"等学术大展评委。承担教育部社科规划项目两项、广东省社科项目一项。出版专著及编著 9 种，在《文艺研究》、《美术》、《美术研究》、《美术观察》等国家级刊物上发表文章 120 余篇，其中"20 世纪中国版画的语境转换"获首届美术学奖（论文）一等奖，《中国新兴版画发展史》获省社科优秀成果（著作）一等奖，日本日中文化艺术交流会金奖，及中国版画家协会颁发的"鲁迅版画奖"。

Qi Fengge

Qi Fengge ,Qi graduated from The Faculty of Fine Art in The North-Eastern Normal University in 1974. In 1982 he graduated from The Chinese Language Department of the same university and between 1988-1990 was assigned to Japan for further study. In 1992 Qi was promoted to the status of Professor.

In 1993 The Chinese State Council awarded Qi the State Council promulgated Government Special Subsistence. He was appointed to the post of Dean of The Faculty of Fine Arts in The North-Eastern Normal University, a Supervisor for research in Fine Art at MA level and Deputy-Chair of The Jilin Provincial Artist's Association.

Qi Fengge is currently the Dean of Shenzhen University, Academy of Art and Design, Professor, Deputy-Director of The Chinese Artist's Association Printmaking Committee and Editor–in-Chief of the journal 'China Printmaking'.

Qi was appointed to the Selection Committee of the 8th, 9th and 10th National Printmaking Exhibition, the 14th,15th and 16th National Printmaking Exhibition and The Beijing International Printmaking Exhibition, ' China Fine Arts Today' and other major academic exhibitions.

Qi also assumed the role of responsibility for the Education Bureau's Social Science Programme in two of its elements and for one element of the Guangdong Social Science Programme.

Qi has published in nine areas of monographs and writing, in ' Research in Literature and Art' , ' Fine Art' , 'A Survey of Fine Art' and in other national level publications with a total of more than 120 articles, among which are 'Context and Change in 20th century Chinese Printmaking' which was awarded First Prize (Dissertation) in The First Prize for the Study of Fine Art. His paper 'The History and Development of New Printmaking in China' was awarded First Prize in the Provincial Social Science Outstanding Achievements (Writer), the Gold Medal from the Japanese Japan-China Culture in the Arts Exchange Association and 'The Lu Xun Printmaking Prize' promulgated by The Chinese Printmaker's Association.

齐凤阁
Qi Fengge

中国版画的承传及拓展

齐凤阁

中国是版画的发源国，是木刻版画的故乡，其悠久的历史传统与开宗拓创之功，已被国际学界所公认。到了现当代，中国版画又异军突起，以其庞大的创作队伍与独特的民族风格及丰硕的艺术成果，赢得"版画大国"的称誉。虽然在有的对科技依赖性强的小版种中，与发达国家比尚有一定差距，但就木版画或整体而言，版画大国的实力与优势是无与伦比的。

我国复制版画的源流要上溯到二千余年前。鲁迅先生说："世界上版画出得最早的是中国"。但早至何年，至今说法不一。过去，一些学者往往把雕版印刷术的发明与版画的创始相联系，其实，在雕版印刷术发明之前，版画技法已在织物印刷及刻印中使用，李平凡先生认为："汉代肖形印的出现和汉代织物印刷图像的应用，实际上已经形成了我国版画最初的创始样式。"①汉代的肖形印，刻制原理与版画相似，所刻禽鸟、龙虎等图像生动、形象，有人就称其为"最古的版画小品"。而汉代画像石刻，由于镂刻与　印效果与版画有相同之处，也曾被人称为"最古的大型版画"。湖南长沙马王堆汉墓出土文物中的"泥金银印花"和"印花敷彩"的织物印刷品，也可谓一种工艺版画，因为前者也是用雕刻的凸版印刷，后者是在印好的图样中用色彩描绘，类似现代的笔彩版画。再有1959年10月，新疆民丰县沙漠古墓中发现的汉代印有图案和人物半身像的蓝色印花布残片，也是用版画技法印制的，这些都说明：我国在制纸术尚未发明或普及之前，版画技术与纺织工艺版画已经出现，之后，随着制纸术的发明，版画的领域不断扩大和发展。

至唐代，木刻版画已开始普及，从唐代的《陀罗尼经咒》、《金刚经》及扉画与《菩萨像》等版画可看出，当时木刻佛画大量产生，不仅有单页佛像，而且有佛经扉画，线条工细，印刷也较讲究，无疑当时已有了专门刻印工匠与作坊。唐代佛教的盛行推动了雕版印刷及复制木刻的发展，而雕版印刷与复制版画又促进了佛教的传播。

两宋金元，是我国复制木刻全面发展的时期。随着小农经济的繁荣，小所有者文化生活的需求，以及民俗文学的发展，木刻的应用范围扩大，不仅表现宗教内容，而且用来刻印各种书籍的附加插图，如南宋刊本《列女传》及元至治年间的《全相生活五种》等通俗文艺性书籍都有优美的插图，一些实用性的书籍如《营造法式》、《重修本草》、《饮膳正要》等，也都附有大量的木刻插图。这说明木刻版画已逐渐从宗教束缚下解放出来，具有了世俗性，并不断得到普及，以满足各阶层人们的需求。尽管有些实用性的书籍插图艺术水平不高，显得粗略不精，但就整体而言，此期的绘、刻都日趋精良，并且出现了木版年画及简单的两版套色版画。从《梅花喜神谱》这样的画谱专辑和一些文艺性书籍插图以及《弥勒菩萨坐像》等佛教版画来看，宋元的木刻已达到了一个前所未有的新水平，内容丰富，风格多样，应用广泛，为明代木刻的更大发展拓宽了道路。

如果说宋元是木刻的发展期，那么，明代则是木刻版画的鼎盛阶段。从经济方面看，明代资本主义生产关系已开始萌芽，工商业的兴起，促进了雕版手工业的发展。从文化方面看，市民文学愈益繁荣，戏曲、小说、唱本、传奇盛极一时，书商为吸引读者，推销刊本，便大量附加木刻插图，当时流行的曲本《西厢记》插图多至数十种，而《三国演义》中的版画竟有240幅之多。可见，文学为木刻版画提拱了广阔的用武之地。

插图书籍的商品化，有力地刺激着雕版印刷手工业的发展，书商的竞争，促使绘刻技艺不断提高。明三百年间，涌现出一批从事雕版的专门人才，而且形成了不同的风格流派。突出的有福建的建安派、江苏的金陵派、安徽歙县的新安派（徽派）。此外，北京、杭州等地也都有众多的刻工终生从事雕版事业，钻研雕刻技巧，在长期的实践中，在激烈的竞争中，使雕版技术达到了纯熟的境地。尤其是当时的一些知名画家，如仇英、唐寅、陈洪绶等也为雕版绘画，他们与雕刻名手分工合作，这便大大提高了木刻版画的艺术质量。从流传下来的明代大量作品可知，就技巧而论，远胜宋元，尤其明中叶以后，刻法细密，风格工丽，更臻成熟。在人物塑造上，不仅比例趋于准确，而且能细致地刻画出不同人物的性格特征及精神面貌。

明代木刻的繁荣。不仅表现在数量多，绘刻精，而且表现在彩印技术上。在这之前，木刻还无力复制彩色绘画，元代的套印也只有朱墨两色，而在明代，分版套印的方法被广泛应用，特别是明末发明的饾版术，是世界彩色印刷的首创。根据画稿分刻成若干板，按原稿的深浅、浓淡施以不同色彩，最后印成色彩缤纷的图画。明末文人胡正言印造的《十竹斋画谱》便用此法印成，后来他又将饾版和拱花两法结合，印刷了《十竹斋笺谱》。从此，使用木刻复制绚丽多彩的图画成为可能，其复制的精到、毕肖，几可乱真。

在我国木刻版画进入盛期之际，欧洲木刻版画才刚刚起步，而且是"从中国学去的，其时是十四世纪初"。据鲁迅先生考证：最初可能是中国学印着极粗的木板图画的纸牌，走进欧洲大陆，成了他们印刷术的祖师②。欧洲现存最早的木刻，是德国十五世纪初的圣母像，比中国的木刻版画要晚得多。

遗憾的是，当木刻版画传到欧洲，在那里迅速发展之时，中国的木刻则在清代后期开始衰落。清初殿刻中的《万寿盛典图》、《南巡盛典图》等，虽一味迎合帝王趣味，为其树碑立传，但还有相当的艺术价值与历史价值。民刻版画，成就亦较突出，其中大画家萧云从的《离骚图》和《太平山水图》，继武之的《芥子园画传》等，均为此时典范，具有较高的艺术性。尤其是木版年画颇为盛行，于十七、十八世纪的明清之间达到了高峰，在整个版画史上，也占有突出的一页。但就整体而言，木刻版画的发展清不如明，清统治者以"诲淫诲盗"为理由的禁书运动，打击了戏曲小说，阻碍了插图艺术的发展，尤其是清中期以后，随着外国列强的侵入，铜版和石印等新印刷术兴起，当时的许多书籍不再用木刻插图，使得木刻版画衰微不振。

任何画种都要经历由盛到衰的过程，这是事物发展的必然。中国古代的复制木刻虽然走完了它的历史行程，默默地消逝于清末民初的艺坛（清末只有荣宝斋等个别书画复制机构经营木版水印业务），但在漫长的历史发展中形成了自己的民族传统，尤其在形式技巧方面，为后代画家酿造了取之不竭的养分，也为创作木刻版画的发生发展提供了必要的条件。

现代的创作版画，以迥异于古代复制版画的崭新姿态，映现了现、当代中国的现实生活，表现了现、当代中国人的审美心态和感情世界，以新的题材内容，新的人物形象，新的形式风格，开始了版画的新时代。所以，人们称之为"新兴版画"。

1931 年至 1937 年，是中国创作版画的童年期。其实，在此前还有一段孕育过程，据吴梦非在《"五四"运动前后的美术教育回忆片断》中记述，民国之初，浙江第一师范的学生业余艺术团体乐石社，在教师李叔同的指导下曾刻过木刻，并印过一本《木版画集》，只是今天无法看到。据朱光潜回忆，二十年代初丰子恺也刻过木刻。特别是从二十年代末开始鲁迅先生有计划地介绍外国创作版画，成为中国新兴版画兴起的先导。1931 年 6 月，创作木刻在第二次一八艺社习作展览会上公开出现，此后，新兴木刻便以战斗姿态，以现实主义的批判精神，投入了反帝、反封建的革命洪流，并成为革命美术的先锋队，但就艺术的表现形式而言，童年期属于模仿阶段，存在着严重的欧化倾向，没有形成民族特色。

从 1937 年直至 1949 年中华人民共和国成立，属于创作版画的成长期。抗日战争的爆发，使新兴版画运动发生了重大转折，首先，版画作者从狭小的亭子间走出，奔赴战区和农村，参加实际斗争，接触劳动群众。这一举动，在两方面促进了版画的发展，一是对表现对象及其生活的熟悉了解，使作品的内涵更加充实深刻，人物形象也较以前真实生动，二是在与服务对象的接触中，审美情趣开始接近，大众化、民族形式等问题更受重视并渐趋解决。单从艺术表现形式上讲，这是由欧化向民族化的转变时期，特别是解放区的版画，1942 年后，在毛泽东《在延安文艺座谈会上的讲话》精神指引下，不仅确立了民族风范，改变了欧化倾向，而且在题材内容上，表现重大的历史变革，描绘解放区的新生活，使新兴版画的面貌发生了重大变化。

1949 年至 1966 年，是创作版画的成熟期。新中国的建立，为新兴版画的发展开辟了广阔前景，虽然也不断受到极左思潮的冲击与干扰，但已不像战争年代那样，要求版画紧紧与政治运动结合，此时期的版画开始注重自身的独立性和审美价值。另外版画家的专业化，也有利于版画艺术水准的提高，即使在大专院校或出版部门工作的版画家，也都是边搞版画教学、研究，边从事版画创作所以出现了一批有个性、有特色的作品，显示了画家的成熟。此时期画家的个性化、风格化，以及不同地区画派的形成，是新兴版画成熟的重要标志。

1966年至1976年"文化大革命"的十年是创作版画的中衰期。由于政治动乱，版画家大部分受到冲击，失去了安定的创作环境与心态，有些人甚至失去了人身自由，致使版画衰落。"文革"后期有些版画家创作了一些作品，但很难与观众见面。工农兵版画的兴起，是此时版画的一大特征，但除极少较好作品外，多数水准平平，有些尚未进入艺术的层面。

1977年至今为全面发展期。其实1977与1978两年是过渡阶段，真正的转折是在1979年改革开放以后。新时期的改革开放，开阔了人们的视野，更新了版画家的观念，有利于艺术繁荣发展的文化政策与氛围，使版画创作由原来的单一封闭型转化为多样开放型，重构了版画格局。所谓全面发展，不单指版画的不同风格、视觉形象的多样并存互补，而且体现于版材、版种、工艺技法的多样性，以及创作主体的多层次。从纵向角度看，新时期版画连接过去，又指向未来，是建国后十七年版画的继承与变革性发展，又是向新世纪过渡的历史起点。

如今，中国的创作版画经历了五个阶段，已有七十余年的历史，走出了它蹒跚学步的童年期，度过了横枪跃马的青年时代，由稚嫩走向成熟，由中衰又进入繁盛阶段。这七十年，我国发生了翻天覆地的变化，版画像一部伟大的史诗，形象地记录了中国人民火热的斗争、壮丽的生活，七十年的创作版画史，也像一首新老画家合奏的交响乐，激昂、雄壮，也有舒缓悠扬的旋律，这是一段风采动人、又内涵丰富的美的历程。

本集收入的16位版画家的不同时期的作品，体现了老中青三代不同的艺术追求与审美轨迹，虽然无法涵盖浩如烟海的中国现代版画的全貌，但在风格探索的广度、艺术语言锤炼的精度，以及媒材、技艺的包容性等方面，都有相当的代表性。

【注释】
① 《李平凡文集》第136页，福建美术出版社1993年出版。
② 鲁迅《〈近代木刻选集〉一小引》。

Qi Fengge

China is the nation in which printmaking originated, it is the ancient home of woodcut printmaking, its' long historical tradition and early achievements in the invention of printmaking have already been generally recognised in international academic circles. Coming into the contemporary period, Chinese printmaking is also a new force coming to the fore, with its huge creative ranks and characteristic national styles, as well as rich artistic success, China has gained the title of ' the great nation of printmaking'. Despite the reliance on etching and lithography in relation to the kinds of small blocks used in woodcut printmaking, there is still a definite gap in esteem compared to developed countries, nevertheless with woodblock printmaking taken overall, the strength and superiority of ' the great nation of printmaking' is without equal.

The source and flow of China's reproductive printmaking can be traced back more than two thousand years. Lu Xun said 'in the world, China was the country which saw the earliest emergence of printmaking'. Yet which was this earliest year, until now the arguments have been numerous. In the past, several scholars have often made the invention of the art of printing from cut wooden blocks and the origin of printmaking appear related, in fact, before the invention of printing from cut wooden blocks printmaking techniques had already been used in the printing of fabrics and the cutting of seals, Li Pingfan considers 'with the emergence of pictorial seals in the Han dynasty and the use during the Han dynasty of fabrics showing printed images, in practice these printed materials had already formed the earliest original form of printmaking in China'. ① In the Han dynasty pictorial seals the cutting principles appear to be the same as those in printmaking, the cut birds, dragons, tigers and other pictorial images, some people have referred to these as 'the most ancient small works of printmaking'. More so Han dynasty pictorial stone cuts, which as a result of their cut and dab printed effects having similarities with printmaking, have also been named by some as 'the oldest large scale examples of printmaking'. The ' gold and silver empasto patterned' and 'printed patterns with hand painted colour' printed fabrics excavated with other antiquities from the Han dynasty tomb at Mawangdui in Changsha, Hunan; can also be called a kind of industrialised printing, because the former also used wooden blocks cut in relief for printing, the latter is in finely printed patterns drawn in colour, similar in category to present day hand coloured prints. Yet again there are the Han dynasty patterns and half length figures on blue printed fragments of fabric discovered in the ancient desert tombs of Minfeng county, Xinjiang in October 1959 that used printing techniques in their manufacture, these can all be explained. Before the art of the making of paper had been completed or made popular in China, printmaking techniques and the arts of printing on spun and woven fabrics had emerged, later, following the invention of the manufacture of paper, the realm of printmaking continually expanded and developed.

By the Tang dynasty printing from cut wooden blocks had already begun to be more extensively used, from the Tang dynasty ' Mantras of the Dharani', 'The Diamond Sutra' and the frontispiece for 'The Image of the Bodisattva' and other prints it is possible to see the large scale woodcut printed Buddhist images coming into being during that time, not only single sheet Buddhist images but also printed frontispieces to Buddhist sutras expressed in line worked in great detail, the printing also having been carefully considered. Without doubt there were already specialist cutting and printing artisans and workshops. The popularity of Buddhist teachings during the Tang dynasty was given impetus by printing from wooden blocks and the development of reproductive woodcut printmaking, moreover printing from wooden blocks and reproductive woodcut printmaking also helped to accelerate the spread of commentaries on the Buddhist classics. The Northern and Southern Song dynasties, the Jin and the Yuan dynasties was a time of wide ranging development in the reproductive woodcut China. Following the flourishing of the small scale peasant economy and the demands of the cultural life of small land holders together with the development of folk literature the scope of the woodcut expanded, not only in expressing religious content but in the addition of woodcut printed illustrations to all kinds of publications. For example 'The Biographies of Virtuous Women' published during the Southern Song dynasty and 'The fully illustrated five aspects of life' published during the zhizhi period of the Yuan Dynasty between 1321-1327 and other popular literary publications all of which included fine illustrations. Several practical publications like 'The Treatise on Architectural Methods' published around 1100, 'The revised Materia Medica', 'The Standards and Principles of Eating and Drinking' and others, all of which also contained a great many woodcut printed illustrations. This demonstrates that woodcut printmaking had already become gradually liberated from religious strictures, sharing common customs and continuously achieving universal popularity by satisfying people's needs at every level of society. Even though there were several practical publications where the level of illustrative skills were low, appearing rough and unrefined, yet taken overall, the images of the time, with each day passing were cut with the best of qualities, moreover woodcut printed New Year pictures and simple two block printed colour prints emerged. From 'The Joyous Spirit of the Plum Blossom', published in 1261, the specialised compilations of this style of picture manual and several illustrated literary publications including 'An image of the seated Maitreya Bodhisattva' and other Buddhist prints seen as examples, the Song and Yuan dynasty's woodcuts had already arrived at an unprecedented new level. The content was rich, with stylistic variety, the usage extensive, widening the road for the even greater development of the woodcut during the Ming dynasty. For example if one suggests that the Song and Yuan dynasties were the period of the development of the woodcut, in that case then the Ming dynasty was the period of full bloom. Looking at it from the economic point of view, the Ming dynasty's capitalist production relationship had already started to bud, the rise of industry and commerce accelerated the development of the artisanal skills of block-cutting. From the cultural viewpoint, the literature of the townspeople profited and flourished, operatic libretti, novels, books of song verses, commentaries on those of legend were in fashion. Booksellers, in order to attract the readers and to promote their publications, caused a great many woodcut illustrations to be added, the illustrations to the contemporary volume of popular operatic libretti 'The Story of the Western Chamber ' could be found in more than ten different versions and in 'The Romance of the Three Kingdoms' eventually contained more then two hundred and forty illustrations. It is possible to see that literature provided the basis for a wide range of usage for the woodcut printed image.

The commercialisation of illustrated publications had a powerful, stimulating influence on the development of the artisanal craft of printing from cut wooden blocks, the competition among booksellers impelled a ceaseless raising of drawing and cutting skills. During the three hundred years of the Ming dynasty groups of people with specialist skills engaged in the cutting of blocks emerged in great numbers, furthermore forming themselves into different stylistic schools; the Jinling school in Jiangsu, the Xin'an school of She county in Anhui known as the Hui school. Apart from these, Beijing, Hangzhou and other places also had numerous artisan block-cutters who spent their entire lives engaged in the practice of cutting blocks, intently studying the skills of block cutting over their long period of practice, in a wave of competition, causing the arts of block cutting and printing to achieve conditions of great skill. Several well known artists of the time, Qiu Ying, Tang Yin, Chen Hongshou and others drew images for woodcut prints, they and the famous woodblock cutters divided the work to complete the task, this greatly raised the quality of the woodblock printmaking arts. From the great number of extant works known to have come down to us from the Ming dynasty the skills may be evaluated as far surpassing those of the Song and Yuan dynasties and especially after the blossoming of the mid-Ming, the cutting techniques were fine and meticulous, the style beautifully worked yet even more importantly attaining maturity.

In the modelling of the figures not only do the proportions tend towards being correct they are moreover meticulously pictorialised in the cutting, the dispositional characteristics and spiritual features of the different figures.

The woodcut flourished during the Ming dynasty. Not only was it expressed in great numbers, with fine drawing and cutting, but expressed in colour printing techniques. Before this time the woodcut was still unable to reproduce colour images, the multi-block printing of the Yuan dynasty was only capable of printing in the two colours of vermilion and black, yet in the Ming dynasty the methods of multi-colour printing by separating out and cutting the different colours onto different blocks came into widespread use, especially so with the invention of 'douban' printing towards the end of the Ming dynasty, the first creative use of colour printing in the world.

According to the demands of the preparatory drawing, the image was separated up into its different colours and cut onto a certain number of blocks, making reference to the tones of colour of the original, with dark and light being shown as different colours, the image finally being printed in a profusion of colours. The late Ming literati Hu Zhengyan used this method in his printing of 'The Ten Bamboo Album of Calligraphy and Painting', later he would also combine together the techniques of 'douban' printing and dry embossing in his ' Ten Bamboo Album of Letter Papers'. From then on the use of woodcut reproduction to achieve sumptuous multi-colour images became possible, the precision of its reproduction, its close resemblance to the original, who could say which was the original.

During the time that China's woodcut printmaking was entering its period of flowering, European woodcut printing was only just beginning, moreover it was 'in mimicry of China', being from the early 14th century. According to Lu Xun's analysis : 'the earliest is perhaps a mimicry of a Chinese playing card, a crudely printed woodcut image, which having entered Europe's great land mass became the founder of their printing arts.' ② The earliest extant woodcut in Europe is the early 15th century German image of the Virgin Mary, very late when compared to China's woodcut prints.

The pity is, just as woodcut printmaking reached Europe, a time of rapid development there, China's woodcuts were, in the later Qing period, beginning to decline. In the early Qing, the Palace Edition of 'An Illustration of the Grand Ceremony of Longevity' and 'An Illustration of the Grand Ceremony of the Southern Tour' although pandering to the Emperor's interest in building up his public image, still have considerable artistic and historical value.

The achievement of folk woodcut prints has by comparison been outstanding, among which works by the great artist Xiao Yuncong such as his 'Images of Encountering Sorrow' and 'Images of Taiping Landscapes', Ji Wuzhi's work ' The Mustard Seed Garden Manual of Painting' and others are without exception exemplars of the time, having a comparatively high level of artistry. Particularly so the rather voguish New Year woodcut prints, from the 17th to the 18th centuries of the Ming and Qing period New Year prints reached their peak, in the full history of printmaking they occupy an outstanding page. Yet in the overall development of printmaking the Qing period was inferior to the Ming. On the grounds of a supposed 'propagation of pornography and violence' the Qing rulers initiated a movement to proscribe books, attacking operatic libretti and novels in hindrance of the development of the illustrative arts. This is particularly so after the mid-Qing period following the invasion of the Great Powers of the foreign countries when etching and lithography and other printing skills sprung up, many publications of that time no longer used woodblock printed illustrations,sending woodblock printing into a decline endured without a flutter. Whatever the kind of picture, they will all take the course from their flowering to decline, this is inevitable in the development of things. Although the period of the antique Chinese reproductive woodcut is now over the passage of its history was to quietly fade away from art circles in the period of the late Qing to the beginning of the Nationalist period (the late-Qing period had just the Rong Bao Zhai workshop and individual businesses engaged in the reproduction of calligraphy and painting through woodcut printing with water-soluble inks). But in the very long passage of historical development printmaking formed its own national traditions, especially so in the area of stylistic skills, making for future generations of artists an inexhaustible source of nutrition and providing essential conditions for the development of printmaking.

Contemporary creative printmaking, by taking a totally different stance from that of antique reproductive printmaking, reflects the here and now, the realities of life in contemporary China, expressing the contemporary Chinese people's appreciation of intellectual beauty and their emotional worlds by its content of new material, new figurative forms and new forms of style begnning a new period for printmaking, referred to by people as 'the new printmaking'.

The period between 1931 and 1937 was the childhood of China's creative printmaking. In fact, before this time there was a period of gestation. Wu Mengfei in his 'Fragmentary recollections of art education before and after the May 4th Movement' records, at the beginning of the Nationalist era, the first teacher training fine art group of part –time students in Zhejiang, the Leshishe (The Society of the Joyous Stone) began to make woodcuts under the direction of their teacher Li Shutong, they printed a book entitled 'A Collection of Woodcut Prints', only it is impossible to find this book today. According to Zhu Guangqian's recollections, Feng Zikai also made woodcuts at the beginning of the twentieth century. Particularly so as from the end of the twentieth century, as Lu Xun had planned, began an introduction to the creative prints from overseas countries, becoming the rising guide to China's new printmaking. In June 1931, in the second 18 Art Society's exhibition of drawings and compositions, creative printmaking emerged onto the public stage. Following this, new printmaking took on a war stance, with a realistic and critical spirit it threw itself into an anti-imperialist and anti-feudalist mighty revolutionary torrent, becoming the vanguard of revolutionary art. Yet, it may be said that the childhood period of this artistic form of expression belonged to the imitative stage, held back by a grave tendency towards westernisation, not having the forms of national characteristics.

The period from 1937 until 1949 and the establishment of the Peoples' Republic of China, coincided with the period of the maturing of creative printmaking. The outbreak of the anti-Japanese war led the new printmaking movement to an important turn of events, in the first place, the makers of prints left their narrow and small garrets to rush to the areas of battle and to the countryside, to take part in the realities of struggle, making contact with the working masses. This event, in two aspects promoted the development of printmaking; the first is to express targets as well as their familiar understanding of life, causing the content of the work to be even more substantial and profound, the figurative images also more realistic and truly dynamic compared with earlier ones, the second is in the contact with the masses, the appeal of an appreciation of beauty starting to draw closer to the masses, popularisation, a Chinese style and other questions even receiving serious attention and gradually becoming resolved. Only from the artistic style, this is the period of the change over from westernisation to nationalism, particularly the prints from the liberated areas, after 1942, under Mao Zedong's spiritual direction (in the speech for the Yan'an Forum on the Arts and Literature) was not only established the manner of the national style but the tendency towards westernisation was reformed, moreover in the content of the subject matter, major historical changes were expressed, drawing new life into the liberated areas, causing major changes to the face of the new printmaking.

The period from 1949 until 1966 was the time during which creative printmaking matured. The establishment of new China opened up a broad foreground for the development of creative printmaking whilst receiving a pounding and disturbances from ultra-left trends of thought; unlike the war period when art was required to closely reflect political movements, the prints of this period began to lay stress on the value of their own individuality and aesthetic sensibilities. Besides this, the specialisations of printmakers were also of benefit in the raising of standards within the printmaking arts, the work of printmakers in the specialised academies or those working in publishing and to all those engaged in the teaching of printmaking, in research or working in creative printmaking also benefited from the emergence of individualism and character in their works, the raising of standards and the emergence of individualism both displayed printmaking's maturity. In this time period the individualism of artists, their style, as well as in the styles of the schools of artists in different places, were the most important symbols of the maturity of the new printmaking.

The years from 1966 until 1976, the ten years of 'the great proletarian cultural revolution' were the period of semi-decline for printmaking, due to the disorder in the government the majority of printmakers were subjected to abuse, loosing the stability of their creative environments and mind, several persons even went so far as to loose their liberty resulting in the decline of printmaking. In the period towards the end of the 'cultural revolution' there were a few printmakers who made a few works but it was very difficult for people to see them. The rise of the worker, peasant, soldier prints is one of the features of this period of printmaking, yet apart from a very few good works the majority were mediocre, some did not even merit being regarded as on a level with fine art.

The time since 1977 has been a period of widespread development. Particularly so during the two years 1977 and 1978 which were a time of transition, the real turn of events was in 1979 after the 'open door' policies had come into effect. A new period of reforms had come into blossom, widening the people's field of vision, even renewing printmaker's ideas, the policies having benefits in the cultural policies and atmosphere of fine art's flourishing development, causing the creativity of printmakers to change from its original single, sealed mould into a multi-styled open form which re-established printmaking's structure. The so called overall development did not impose a single direction on printmaking's different styles, visual images took many forms and retained mutual benefits, moreover reflected in the materials of block, the kind of block and the multiplicity of working methods as well as the many levels of the creative subject. From the vertical point of view, the printmaking of the new era linked with the past and also pointed to the future, it is the inheritance of the printmaking of the period seventeen years after the founding of the state and its changing development, it is also an historical starting point in the transition towards the new century.

Today, China's creative printmaking has passed through five stages in its history, having already more than seventy years of history, it has gone through its limping learning to walk childhood period, its youth spent galloping ahead with rifles at the ready, from young and tender towards maturity, from decline to a period of its thriving. Earthshaking changes have occurred in China during these seventy years, printmaking's appearance is like a part of a grand historical poem, seemingly recording the Chinese people's fiery struggle, glorious life, seventy years of creative printmaking's history, also seeming like some first symphonic music from a combination of new and elderly printmakers, impassioned and majestic, also having a leisurely, rising and falling melody, this is part of a strikingly elegant and graceful bearing which has also followed a richly beautiful course.

This collection of the work of sixteen artists from different times embodies the artistic pursuits and aesthetic orbits of three generations of elderly, middle aged and young printmakers, although unable to contain a complete picture of contemporary Chinese printmaking, yet in the scope of stylistic expression, the precision of its hammering into shape of the artistic language as well as the materials of media, skill content and other aspects all have appropriate representation.

Notes:

①. Li Pingfan collected essays' p.136. Fujian Fine Art Press 1993

②. Lu Xun (A selection of recent woodcuts- short quotations)

大卫巴克

学术背景

1966	取得伦敦大学艺术系学士学位
1967	取得伦敦大学艺术系教师资格
1995	皇家学会版画家协会名誉会员
1997	鲁迅艺术学院名誉教授
2002	中国国家研究院名誉教授
2005	阿尔斯特大学退休高级讲师

导师工作

担任哲学系博士生导师（已有 3 个学生完成学业 ,2 个正在学习）

研究方向

中国版画的历史、技术和术语

学术实践

伦敦 Sotheby 艺术研究院的客座讲师

中国国家研究院的客座教授

《今日版画》咨询部的成员

英国图书馆中国版画派系成员

中国国家研究院国际交流委员会成员

研究成果

2002	AHRB	主要科研奖
2000	AHRB	小型科研补助金

即将出版作品

2006　陈琦－木版画　1983－2005

　　　伦敦木版基金会 将在伦敦 Bankside 画廊展览 2006 年 7 月出版

2006　黄家绘刻刻木

　　　伦敦木版基金会 AHRB Funded

大卫巴克
David Barker

发表作品

2005 艺术解放——中国深圳桃源小学使用聚苯乙烯板的版画教学

　　　　翻译和编辑《今日版画》14 册第 3 章 26—27 页 ISSN 0960—9253

2005 中国传统印花台板的评论

　　　　这篇文章发表于 Sotheby 的艺术研究院的 2005 年伦敦亚洲周上，当日

　　　　的研究题目是"中国 18 世纪单页印刷的技术、表达思想和市场"

2005 当代版中的传统技术

　　　　A&C Black，London ISBN 0—7136—6409—6

2005 黑土地颂歌

　　　　黑龙江省当代版画展览 收藏于普通话协会画册

2005 王超，近期创作的木版印刷书和木版画

　　　　收藏于阿尔斯特大学 ISBN 1—8592—3190—X

2004 整体，自觉，探索

　　　　《中国版画》2003 年 22 期范敏发表的一篇文章的翻译和校对

　　　　《今日版画》第 13 册第 3 章 26—27 页 ISSN 0960—9253

2003 中国版画的发展和前景

　　　　《今日版画》第 12 册第 4 章 5—7 页 ISSN 0960—9253

2003 中国版画新的前景 1980—2002

　　　　翻译和编辑，《中国今日版画》 伦敦英国图书馆 ISBN 0—7123—4823—9

2003 1980—2000 的中国木版画

　　　　《中国今日版画》 英国图书馆，伦敦 ISBN 0—7123—4823—9

2003 木版基金会：理想和愿望

　　　　《中国今日版画》 英国图书馆，伦敦 ISBN 0—7123—4823—9

2003 中国木版画相关的英文——中文词汇表

　　　　《当代中国木版画艺术》 伦敦木版基金会 ISBN 0—9546—0481—4

2003 当代中国版画艺术——60 幅版画作品

　　　　伦敦木版基金会

2002 中国和日本彩色印刷设备的关系

　　　　"东亚木版艺术"会议 Somerset House，伦敦

2002 日本木版画

　　　　2001 年日本节巡回展览 ISBN 1—85923—1 594

2002 Yoko Omomi，近期版画作品

　　　　2001 年日本节巡回展览

2001 30 年的版画工作间

　　　　阿尔斯特大学巡回展览 ISBN 1—8592—3151—9

2001 百年印刷

　　　　《今日版画》第 10 册第 1 章第 9 页 ISSN 0960—9253

2001 接触木版画

《今日版画》第 10 册第 1 章第 10 页 ISSN 0960-9253

2001　徽派版画史论集

　　　英国图书馆中国版画派系

2000　改革之后

　　　《今日版画》第 9 册第 3 章 19-20 页 ISSN 0 960 -9253

1999　郑爽版画　　1980-1996

　　　收藏于艺术讨论会巡回展览和阿尔斯特大学 ISBN 1-85923-1152

1998　他们认为中国是一个杯子，俞启慧谈话

　　　《今日版画》第 5 册第 4 章 3-5 页 ISSN 0960-9253

1996　中国版画——丝网印刷的摇篮

　　　《今日版画》第 5 册第 1 章 16-17 页 ISSN 0960-9253

1995　版画英文——中文词汇

　　　阿尔斯特大学贝尔法斯特 ISBN 1-85923-013-X

获奖

1973　Alice-Berger　　Hammerschlag　　传播奖（瑞典）

1981　北爱尔兰艺术委员会主要传播奖（中国）

1986　艺术委员会展览奖（新加坡）

1992　英国委员会传播奖（日本）

1995　英国委员会传播奖（加拿大）

主要展览

1978　第 4 届挪威版画双年展

1980　第 5 届挪威版画双年展

1980　喜悦的目光，伦敦

1980　第 2 届 Listowel 版画双年展

1981　第 1 届雕刻 3 年展，意大利威尼斯

1981　第二届欧洲版画双年展，德国巴登

1982　第六届挪威版画双年展

1982　第 5 届欧洲雕刻双年展，法国牟罗兹

1983　第 3 届 Listowel 版画双年展

1984　世界版画展美国站

1989　个人展，爱尔兰沃特福德

1998　中国深圳艺术画廊

2000　中国重庆版画制作讨论会

David Barker

Academic and Professional Qualifications

1966	BA Fine Art	University of London
1967	Art Teachers Certificate	University of London
1995	Honorary Fellow, Royal Society of Painter-Printmakers	
1997	Honorary Professor, Lu Xun Academy of Fine Art	
2002	Honorary Professor, China National Academy	
2005	Reader Emeritus, University of Ulster	

Supervisory Responsibilities

Doctor of Philosophy (3 successful completing, 2 pending)

Research Interest

The history, technology and terminology of Chinese printmaking

Professional Activities

Visiting Lecturer, Sotheby's Institute of Art, London

Visiting Professor, China National Academy

Member, Advisory Board, 'Printmaking Today'

Member, Chinese Print Circle, British Library

Member, International Exchange Committee, China National Academy

Research Awards

2002   AHRB Major Research Award

2000   AHRB Small Research Grant

Publications pending / in preparation

2006   Chen Qi – Woodblock prints 1983-2005

   The Muban Foundation, London

   for exhibition at the Bankside Gallery, London

   July 2006

2006   The Huang family of illustrative blockcutters

   The Muban Foundation, London

AHRB Funded

Publications

2005   Artistic liberation, the teaching of printmaking using polystyrene

Blocks at Taoyuan Primary School, Shenzhen, China

Translation and edit

Printmaking Today, vol.14 no.3 pp 26-27

ISSN 0960-9253

2005   Some notes on the traditional Chinese printing table

A paper presented at Sotheby's Institute of Art, London for Asia Week 2005

Study day title:

'The sheet print in eighteenth century China technique, image and market'

2005   Traditional Techniques in Contemporary Chinese Printmaking

A&C Black, London

ISBN 0-7136-6409-6

2005   Ode To The Black Earth

An Exhibition of Contemporary Prints from Heilongjiang Province

Catalogue and curation for the Mandarin Speakers Association

2005   Wang Chao, Recent woodblock printed books and single sheet prints

Catalogue and curation for the University of Ulster,

Belfast Print Workshop and Visiting Arts

ISBN 1-8592-3190-X

2004   Wholeness, consciousness, discovery

Translation and edit of an article by Fan Min in China Printmaking, Issue 22 2003

Printmaking Today, vol.13 no.3 pp 26-27

ISSN 0960-9253

2003   Perspective, the evolution of the Chinese woodcut

Printmaking Today, vol.12 no.4 pp 5-7

ISSN 0960-9253

2003   A new outlook for Chinese prints 1980-2002

Translation and edit in 'Chinese Printmaking Today'

The British Library, London

ISBN 0-7123-4823-9

2003   Woodblock Printing in China 1980-2000

In 'Chinese Printmaking Today'

The British Library, London

ISBN 0-7123-4823-9

2003   The Muban Foundation: Ideals and Aspirations

In 'Chinese Printmaking Today'

The British Library, London

ISBN 0-7123-4823-9

2003   English-Chinese Glossary of terms relating to Chinese woodblock printmaking

In 'The Art of Contemporary Chinese Woodcuts',

The Muban Foundation, London

ISBN 0-9546-0481-4

2003   60 Woodcut Prints, The Art of Contemporary Chinese Woodcuts

The Muban Foundation, London

2002   The relationships between Chinese and Japanese colour printing devices

For 'The Woodblock Art in East Asia' Conference,

Somerset House, London

2002   Japanese Woodcut Prints

A touring exhibition and catalogue for Japan Festival 2001

ISBN 1-85923-1594

2002   Yoko Omomi, recent prints

A touring exhibition and catalogue for Japan Festival 2001

2001   30 years of the Printmaking Workshop

A touring exhibition and catalogue for The University of Ulster

ISBN 1-8592-3151-9

2001   Print century

In 'Printmaking Today' vol.10 no.1 p.9

ISSN 0960-9253

2001   Knock on wood

In 'Printmaking Today' vol.10 no.1 p.10

ISSN 0960-9253

2001   The collected history of the prints of the Hui school

A paper for the Chinese Print Circle, British Library

2000   After the Revolution

In 'Printmaking Today' vol.9 no.3 p.19-20

ISSN 0960-9253

1999   Zheng Shuang Woodcuts 1980-1996

A touring exhibition and catalogue for the Arts Council (NI)

and The University of Ulster

ISBN 1-85923-1152

1998 They think of China as sups, Yu Qihui in conversation

In 'Printmaking Today' vol.5 no.4 pp 3-5

ISSN 0960-9253

1996 Printmaking in China, the cradle of screen-printing

In 'Printmaking Today' vol.5 no.1 pp 16-17

ISSN 0960-9253

1995 An English-Chinese Glossary of Printmaking Terms

Belfast, University of Ulster

ISBN 1-85923-013-X

Awards and Prizes

1973 Alice-Berger Hammerschlag Travel Awards (Sweden)

1981 Arts Council of Northern Ireland Major Travel Award (China)

1986 Arts Council Exhibition Award (Singapore)

1992 British Council Travel Award (Japan)

1995 British Council Travel Award (Canada)

Major Exhibitions

1978 4th Norwegian Print Biennale

1980 5th Norwegian Print Biennale

1980 The Delight Eye, London

1980 2nd Listowel Print Biennale

1981 1st Triennale of Engraving, Venice, Italy

1981 2nd European Print Biennale, Baden-Baden, Germany

1982 6th Norwegian Print Biennale

1982 5th European Biennale of Engraving, Mulhouse, France

1983 3rd Listowel Print Biennale

1984 World Print 4, USA Tour

1989 One Person Exhibition, Waterford, Ireland

1998 Shen Zhen Art Gallery, China

2000 Chongqing Printmaking Conference, China

致读者 COMMENTARY

尽管对中国传统和当代版画缺乏研究，西方学术界还是很热衷于认识和了解这项艺术。相对而言，日本版画的历史和技术的研究比较详尽，中国版画虽然拥有自己独特新颖的技术，但类似的研究几乎是空白，其原因是多方面的，诸如中文难以掌握、地理位置距离遥远、政治隔绝、工艺技术方面记载的缺失以及中国近代所经历的苦难，无疑都是造成这种状况的重要影响因素。

中国版画近代史与中国早期的革命史同步，到 20 世纪 30 年代，已经拥有 1300 余年历史的中国版画处在一个转折点上，在鲁迅先生的努力下，中国版画有了新的风格和寓意。从此以后，中国当代版画家可以衡量自己的成就了。这次发起的版画活动规模虽然不是很大，但是通过近期一系列的展览，欧洲艺术家和学者增进了对中国版画的了解并提高了对这项艺术的兴趣。但是研究中国版画的上述制约因素仍然存在，这是一项在丰富资源下才能进行的专门研究，在表面上来看，该项研究没有主要的基金会介入，中国版画的收藏家也相当稀少。这本画册记载了王柏年先生为他的公司——加拿大北美永新能源有限公司所收藏的版画作品，画册不仅仅收藏了 16 位在版画方面取得卓越成就的画家的作品，而且也为其他有相同愿望的人们指出了一种可参考的方法，这是件非常令人称赞的事情。尽管世界各地的老师和工作室不断努力，但是中国版画仍然被错误地认为原始作品是可以复制出多份作品，并且复制品也属于真正的原始作品。去世很久的画家的原始作品和复制品的混淆是很普遍的，但是永新能源这次的行为给予了画家、画家作品原创性显著的信心，同时也给予了像其他视觉艺术一样展示视觉思想的版画制作信心。

我深信，这本画册的问世，会在国际版画界得到认可，因此王柏年先生和他的公司值得每一位画家和版画研究人员的感谢。

大卫巴克

In the western academic field the study of Chinese printmaking in both it's historical and contemporary forms is carried by an enthusiastic but small body of researchers.

Compared to the many detailed studies of neighboring Japanese printmaking history and techniques, similar studies of the unique and original techniques practiced by the Chinese have been sadly lacking, why this is so is complex to explain. Difficulties of language acquisition, geographical distances, political isolation, the lack of substantive records of what was seen as mere craft coupled with the turbulence of recent Chinese history are all certainly contributory factors.

The recent history of Chinese printmaking runs in parallel with the gestation and birth of new china, the efforts of Lu Xun in creating a new language and purpose for the woodcut which, by the 1930s, had already been part of Chinese history for more than 1300 years was a pivotal point in time from which contemporary Chinese printmakers can measure their achievements. With this re-emergence of practice has come a slow but growing understanding and interest by European artists and scholars encouraged by several recent major exhibitions. Whilst some of these difficulties remain, the study of Chinese printmaking is still a highly specialized and under-resourced area with few comprehensive histories and seemingly scant attention from major funding bodies. Collectors of Chinese prints are also conspicuously few, consequently the publication of this catalogue recording the initiative of Pa Wong in acquiring prints for his Company, Novel Energy Ltd., is to be particularly applauded, the catalogue profiling the work of the sixteen artists records not only a fuller recognition of this aspect of China's heritage but sets an example that one hopes others may follow.

Despite the efforts of teachers and workshops worldwide printmaking is still misunderstood in that the nature of original prints can be both multiple and yet genuinely original. The confusion between original printmaking and the reproduction of works from other media by often long dead artists seems regrettably universal, consequently Novel Energy's initiative is significant in showing a clear confidence in both the artists, the originality of their practice and in printmaking's ability to illustrate visual ideas as convincingly as any other medium in the visual arts.

Artists and researchers should be grateful to Pa Wong and to the Company for the greater international recognition of the field this publication will bring.

David Barker

THE ARTISTS AND THEIR WORKS

画家与作品

阿鸽

阿鸽（1948—   ），四川凉山人、彝族。1964 年毕业于四川美术学院。现任四川美术家协会理事、四川省美术馆副馆长、神州版画博物馆馆长、中国美术家协会理事，国家一级美术师。

A Ge (1948-   ), born in Liangshan, Sichuan of the Yi minority peoples.
A Ge graduated from the Sichuan Academy of Fine Arts in 1964. She currently holds the post of Manager of The Sichuan Artist's Association, Deputy-Director of The Sichuan Provincial Museum, Director of The Shenzhou Museum of Printmaking and Manager of The Chinese Artist's Association. A Ge is also a Grade 1 National Artist.

联系电话 Telephone (86) 13808199995

获奖记录

1979 年第五届全国美展一等奖、1983 年第八届全国版画展优秀作品奖、1984 年第六届全国美展铜奖、1994 年第八届全国美展优秀奖、1998 年第十四届全国版画展银奖、1999 年第九届全国美展铜奖、2002 年第十六届全国版画展铜奖、全国少数民族美术作品展优秀奖、挪威国际版画比赛荣誉奖、1999 年获中国版协颁发的"鲁迅版画奖"。

PRIZES AWARDED

1979 The 5th National Exhibition of Fine Art, First Prize

1983 The 8th National Printmaking Exhibition, Prize for Outstanding Work

1984 The 6th National Exhibition of Fine Art, Bronze medal

1994 The 8th National Exhibition of Fine Art, Prize for Outstanding Work

1998 The 14th National Printmaking Exhibition, Silver medal

1999 The 9th National Exhibition of Fine Art, Bronze medal

1999 The Chinese Artist's Association promulgated 'Lu Xun Print Prize'

2002 The 16th National Printmaking Exhibition, Bronze medal

2002 The National Minority People's Exhibition of Fine Art, Prize for Outstanding Work

2002 The Norwegian International Printmaking Competition, Prize of Honour

彝寨喜迎新社员 阿鸽 木刻
The Yi village welcomes the new member
A Ge
Woodcut
76 × 103(cm) 1975

出版记录

《阿鸽版画》、《四川少数民族画家画库 · 阿鸽》。

收藏记录

有 27 件作品被中国美术馆、大英博物馆、日本国际版画博物馆
等收藏。

PUBLICATIONS

Prints by A Ge

A Pictorial Treasury of Sichuan Minority People Artists – A Ge

WORKS IN THE COLLECTIONS OF

More than 27 works in the collections of:

The China Gallery of Fine Art

The British Museum

The International Museum of Printmaking, Japan

故乡　阿鸽　木刻
Former home
A Ge
Woodcut
65 × 65(cm)　1981

画家心语

我从大凉山走出来，那里是我祖辈生活过的地方，是我的故乡。我要用手中的画笔画出那里的山山水水，反映凉山彝族人民的新生活。

ARTIST'S STATEMENT

I walked down from the Daliang mountains, this is the place where my ancestors have always lived, it is my home area. I want to use the brush in my hand to paint those mountains and water, to reflect the new life of the Yi people in the Liang mountains.

小雪　阿鸽　水印木刻
Light snow
A Ge
Woodcut printed with water-soluble colours
42 × 40(cm) 1982

艺术评介

阿鸽是我国女版画家中的优秀代表，是新中国培养出来的彝族第一代女版画家。她17岁以优异成绩从四川美术学院民族班毕业，便被选为四川美协的专业画家，从此与版画结下不解之缘。"文革"后迎来了她创作的高峰期，以一幅幅刻划少数民族女性形象的版画引人瞩目。她以女画家特有的细致和柔情，满怀深情地表现她的彝族姐妹，反映彝族区解放后人民生活的安定、幸福与美好。《鸽子》、《三月》、《小阿依》、《春到凉山》等常以特写式的镜头，集中刻划彝族女性年轻俊美，妩媚动人的青春活力。阿鸽的作品以温馨的情调与秀美的形象见长，格调清新，墨色滋润，加上少数民族富有装饰美的服装头饰，给人以赏心悦目的美感。近年的创作在造型上由具象趋于抽象、半抽象，在中国民族民间艺术语素与现代艺术手法融合中，寻求新的突破。

ARTISTIC APPRECIATION

A Ge is an outstanding representative of China's female printmakers, being the first women printmaker to be fostered by the new China. At seventeen years of age she graduated with excellent results from the Sichuan Academy of Fine Arts Minority Nationalities Class, even being selected by the Sichuan Artists Association as a professional artist, from then on A Ge wove an indissoluble bond with printmaking. After the 'Cultural Revolution' came the time of the peak of her creative work, print by print she makes woodcuts of images focussing on the women of the minority peoples. As a female printmaker her particular meticulousness and tenderness, fully expresses her Yi national ancestry, reflecting the happiness, fortune and stability in the people's lives of the Yi nationality areas since Liberation. The works 'Doves', ' March ', ' Little A Yi ', ' Spring comes to the Liang mountains' and other works, frequently by close up views of heads, are cut to show the beauty of young Yi nationality women, their charming, touching and youthful vitality. A Ge's work is renowned for its warm sentiment and graceful imagery, her style fresh, the colour alive, adding to the rich colourful clothing and head wear of the minority peoples, giving people a feeling of pleasure from the images they see before them. The work of recent years has in its treatment moved from naturalistic to abstract and semi-abstract, forging a link between the unit of language of the folk arts of China's minority peoples and the skills of contemporary arts, to seek a new breakthrough.

姐妹　阿鸽　水印木刻
Sisters
A Ge
Woodcut printed with water-soluble colours
84 × 62(cm) 1984

卖餐具的小姑娘　阿鸽　套色木刻
Little girl selling tableware
A Ge
Multi-colour woodcut
52 × 46(cm)　1982

放学路上　阿鸽　水印木刻
On the road home from school
A Ge
Woodcut printed with water-soluble colours
50 × 35(cm)　1983

鸽子　阿鸽　木刻
Doves
A Ge
Woodcut
82 × 50(cm)　1984

P/A　　鸽子　　（木刻）　82×50厘米　　阿鸽　1984年

小鹅　阿鸽　水印木刻
Gosling
A Ge
Woodcut printed with water-soluble colours
56 × 50(cm)　1986

小兄妹　阿鸽　水印木刻
Little brother and sister
A Ge
Woodcut printed with water-soluble colours
55 × 44(cm)　1987

索玛　阿鸽　水印木刻
Suo Ma
A Ge
Woodcut printed with water-soluble colours
85 × 56(cm)　1989

私语　阿鸽　套色木刻
Confidential talk
A Ge
Multi-colour woodcut
80 × 55(cm)　1990

赛前　阿鸽　套色木刻
Before the match
A Ge
Multi-colour woodcut
72 × 52(cm) 1990

小雨　阿鸽　水印木刻
Light rain
A Ge
Woodcut printed with water-soluble colours
68 × 58(cm) 1991

▶ 雪蒙蒙　阿鸽　水印木刻
Misty snow
A Ge
Woodcut printed with water-soluble
colours
92 × 60(cm) 1998

陈龙

陈龙（1971—　），生于黑龙江，现为中国美术家协会版画艺术委员会委员，黑龙江省版画艺术委员会主任，中国美术家协会会员，黑龙江省美术家协会创作室专职画家。

Chen Long (1971-　), born in Heilongjiang.

In 1993, Chen is a Member of the Chinese Artist's Association Printmaking Committee, Director of the Heilongjiang Provincial Printmaking Committee, Member of the Chinese Artist's Association, the Heilongjiang Provncial Artist's Association's Institute as an artist.

联系电话 Telephone　　(86)13045165614

451-88711310

451-86037129(office)

451-87501580(home)

电子信箱 E-mail　　cqchenlong2003@163.com

1993年全国三版展、版种大展入选、1994年全国第十二届版画展入选、1995年日本国际版画展入选、1996年全国第十三届版画展入选、黑龙江省第六届版画展银奖、1997年波兰克拉科夫国际版画三年展入选、1998年北京国际小版画银奖、黑龙江省版画展金奖、全国第十四届版画展入选、1999年全国第九届美展入选、2000年全国第十五届版画展银奖、中国国际版画双年展（青岛2000）入选、2001年黑龙江省第三届文艺精品工程大奖、2002年全国第十六届版画展银奖、东北三省版画展大奖、黑龙江省第四届文艺精品工程大奖、2003年中国美术"金彩奖"铜奖、北京国际版画双年展银奖、"今日中国"北京美术展入选、2004年全国第十届美展铜奖、英国大英图书馆，中国当代版画展入选、黑龙江第十届美展金奖、2005年韩国道理美术馆《中国美术之今日》入选、第十三届21CICAA国际艺术节入选。

PRIZES AWARDED

1993 The National Exhibitoion of Three Printmaling Techniques, Drawing Prize
1994 The 12th National Printmaking Exhibition, Drawing Prize
1995 The Japan Intermational Printmaking Exhibitionm Drawingth Prize
1996 The 13th National Printmaking Exhibition, Drawing Prize
1996 The 6th Heilongjiang Provincial Printmaking Exhibition, Silver medal
1997 The Krakow International Printmaking Exhibtion, Siover medal
1998 The Beijing International Miniature Print Biennale, Silver Prize
1998 The Heilongjiang Provincial Printmaking Exhibition, Glod medal
1998 The 14th National Printmaking Exhibition, Drawing Prize
1999 The 9th National Exhibition of Fine Art, Drawing Prize
2000 The 15th National Printmaking Exhibition, Siver Pedal
2000 Qingdao International Print Biennale, Drawing Prize
2001 The 3rd Heilongjiang Provincial Treasures of Literature and Art Project, Grand Prize
2002 The 16th National Printmaking Exhibition, Siver medal
2002 The North-East China Three Provinces of Literature and Art Project, Grand Prize
2002 The 4th Beilongjiang Provincial Treasures of Literature and Art Project, Grand Prize
2003 The China Fine Art'Gold Medal', Bronze medal
2003 The Beijing International Printmaking Biennale, Silver medal
2003 The Beijiing Exhibition of Fine Art'Today's China', Drawing Prize
2004 The 10th National Exhibition of Fine Art, Bronze medal
2004 The Contemporary Chinese Printmaking Exhibition, The British Library, Drawing Prize
2004 The 10th Heilongjing Exhibition of Fine Art, Gole medal
2005 The Exhibition'Today's Chinese Fine Art', Korea, Drawing Prize
2005 The 13th 21CICAA International Art Festival, Drawing Prize

丰收的祈祷　陈龙　木版
Praying for a rich harvest
Chen Long
Woodcut
41.5 × 64(cm) 1994

 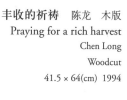

50/50

收藏记录

中国美术馆、英国欧洲木版基金会、北京泰和经典文化交流有限公司、中央美术学院、浙江美术馆、深圳美术馆、广东美术馆、四川神州版画博物馆、安徽省美术馆、江苏美术馆、黑龙江省美术馆、银川美术馆。

出版记录

《陈龙版画作品集》2003 年华文出版社出版。

WORKS IN THE COLLECTION OF

The China Gallery of Fine Art

The Muban Foundation, UK

The Beijing 'Taihe' Scriptures Cultural Exchange Company (Ltd)

The Central Academy of Fine Art

The Zhejiang Gallery of Fine Art

The Shenzhen Gallery of Fine Art

The Guangdong Gallery of Fine Art

The Shenzhou Printmaking Museum, Sichuan

The Anhui Provincial Gallery of Fine Art

The Jiangsu Gallery of Fine Art

The Heilongjiang Provincial Gallery of Fine Art

The Yinchuan Gallery of Fine Art

PUBLICATIONS

'A Collection of Works by Chen Long' 2003
Published by the China Cultural Press

吉祥鄂伦春　陈龙　木版
A lucky Olunchun
Chen Long
Woodcut
44 × 84.5(cm) 1996

画家心语

如何在更为宽泛的领域选择与主体意识更契合的表达方式，使传统方式在现代媒材中充分发挥表现力，全方位的改变传统木刻版画的视觉形态，是我近年来的工作之重。

选择近乎残酷的技术过程，悖论性的否定木版画传统语言外壳，以一种复杂至单纯的观念形态消解技术，摆脱惯性思维方式，使眼睛和思想从意识形态影响中逃脱出来，从而进一步实现木刻版画形态变革，是我当下版画的创作工作的重中之重。

ARTIST'S STATEMENT

How in an even wider-ranging domain to choose and be subject conscious in a corresponding expressive style, to make traditional styles bring their expressive strength fully into play in a contemporary medium, with a multi-directional revision of traditional woodcut printmaking's visual form, this has been my most important task in recent years.

To choose a technical process that is almost brutal, a paradoxical negation of a superficial view of woodcut printmaking's traditional language, through a kind of complicated to simple conceptual form in order to remove technique, to shake off static modes of thinking, to make one's eyes and thinking escape from within a conscious form of influence and from that position to make some progress in realising a reform of woodcut printmaking's form, these are the most important aspect of my current creative work in printmaking.

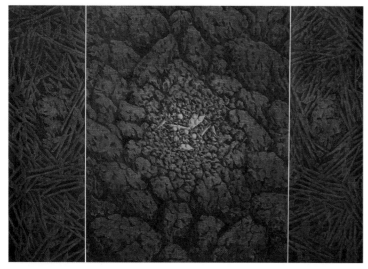

北方秋的延续 1　陈龙　木版
The continuity of the northern autumn I
Chen Long
Woodcut
40 × 70(cm)　1997

陈龙是 20 世纪 90 年代接受学院教育的版画家，他的木刻版画创作是在北大荒开始的，所以在他的作品里依然追求着辽阔、深远的意境，只不过他把那种对现实生活的讴歌转换为对个体生命的关注，把写实再现转换为对心理空间的探求，把套色木刻的一般性语言转换为包含主体精神性的本体语言突现。在他的作品里"大豆"既是具象的植物果实，又是抽象的生命符号。画家将这一生命符号切换配置在幽秘的时空中，从而最大限度地赋予作品以丰富的暗喻性，这种心理空间的表现深度是和他改变北大荒木刻语言唇齿相依的。比如，用精细入微的刻印技术，悖论性的否定传统套色木刻版画的语言外壳，以一种全新的观念消解技术，从而实现对传统木刻版画的超越和现代转换。至 1998 年以来，他的版画作品以其鲜明的图式特征与风貌，强烈的主体意识与精神意蕴不断引起版画界的关注。原因在于他的作品不仅对北大荒前代版画家的创作而言其视觉形态已经发生了根本的变化，而且对于传统木刻版画来说也具有明晰的变革意义，并在视觉形态的转换中不断升华着精神意蕴。

ARTISTIC APPRECIATION

Chen Long is a printmaker who received his academy training in the last decade of the 20th century, his creative work in woodcut printmaking started in the Great Northern Wilderness therefore in his work he is still pursuing its vast and profound moods, he only sings the praises of changes to the realities of that kind of life in order to pay close attention to the lives of individuals, drawing realistically reproduces the changes in order to search after inner spaces, to transform the normal language of the multi-colour woodcut in order to embody the subject matter's spirituality in the advance of a noumenonic language. In his work ' Soya bean' it has both the appearance of a botanical fruit and an abstract symbol for life. The artist has taken this symbol for life deploying it into a secret time and space, thereby the biggest limitation on the task of the work is rich metaphoricism, this inner space's expressive depth is closely related and interdependent on his changes to the language of Beidahuang's woodcut printmaking. For example, using meticulous and subtle cutting and printing techniques, a paradoxical negation of the superficial view of traditional multi-colour woodcut printmaking language, by a wholly new concept to remove technique, thereby realising an overcoming of traditional woodcut printmaking and contemporary changes. From 1998, Chen's prints have become outstanding for their distinctive stylistic character, elegance, strength of subject matter and spiritual meaning continuously touching off close attention to the boundaries of printmaking. The reason lies in Chen's work not only relating to the work of earlier generations of printmakers in Beidahuang but speaks the shape of his visual sense which has already created fundamental changes, moreover it might be said in relation to changes in traditional woodcut printmaking that they have clear reformational implications, as well as in changes to the forms of visual sense continuously raising the level of spiritual significance.

唐风　陈龙　木版
Tang style
Chen Long
Woodcut
22 × 23.4(cm) 2000

梦回赫乡　陈龙　木版
Dreaming of returning to the
Hezhe area
Chen Long
Woodcut
40.5 × 60(cm)　1994

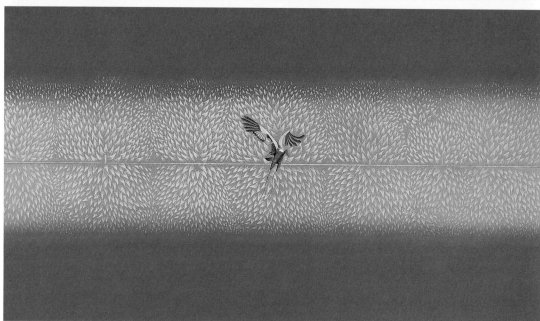

故园秋梦　陈龙　木版
Autumn dream of the old home
Chen Long
Woodcut
40 × 70(cm)　1995

屏风之侍女　陈龙　木版
Maid of the screen
Chen Long
Woodcut
40 × 69.5(cm)　1997

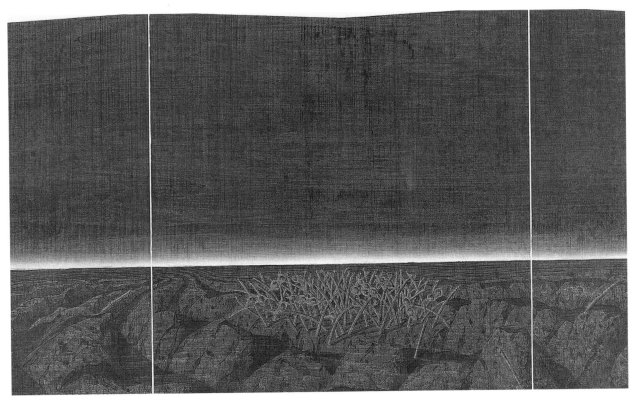

北方的延续 2　陈龙　木版
The continuity of the north II
Chen Long
Woodcut
52 × 80(cm)　1998

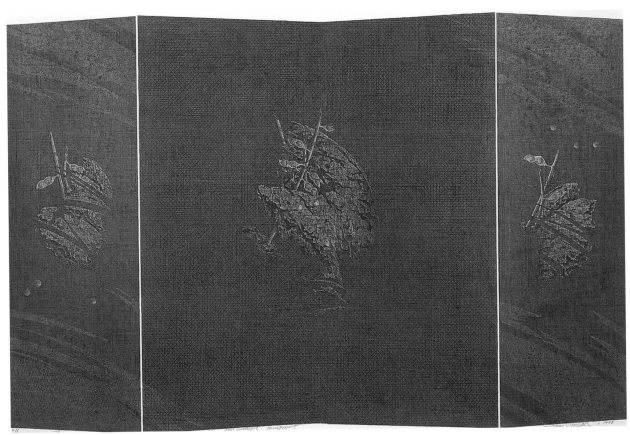

苍土北方　陈龙　木版
The grey soil of the north
Chen Long
Woodcut
66 × 90(cm)　1998

幻入秋的空间　陈龙　木版
An imaginary entering of autumn's space
Chen Long
Wood cut
101 × 60(cm) 1999

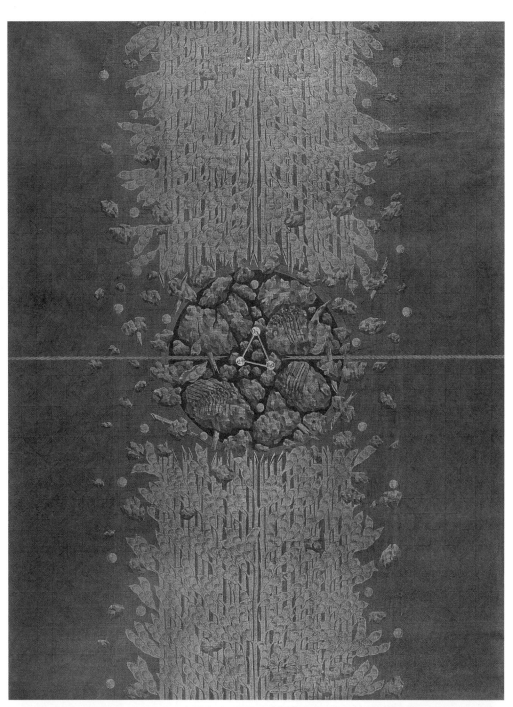

秋的苏生 陈龙 木版
Autumnal revival
Chen Long
Woodcut
90 × 66(cm) 1999

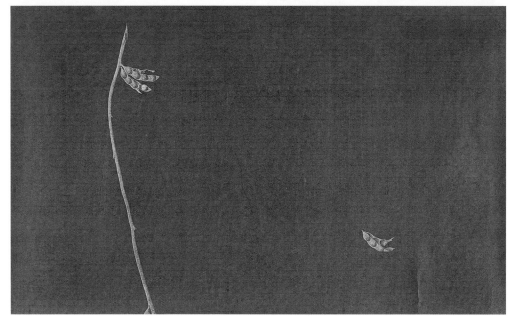

风韵 陈龙 木版
The music of the wind
Chen Long
Woodcut
50 × 90(cm) 2000

遗落荒原的魂 陈龙 木版
Loosing the spirit of the wilderness
Chen Long
Woodcut
90 × 66 (cm) 2000

生之灵 1 陈龙 木版
The spirit of life I
Chen Long
Woodcut
20 × 12(cm) 2001

生之灵 2 陈龙 木版
The spirit of life II
Chen Long
Woodcut
20 × 12(cm) 2001

范敏

范敏 (1963—)，生于辽宁省辽阳市，1988 年吉林艺术学院美术系版画专业毕业，获学士学位，1993 年中央美术学院版画系助教研修班硕士课程班结业，2001 年韩国弘益大学研究院版画系毕业，获美术学硕士学位。现为中国版画家协会会员，天津美术学院版画系主任、副教授。

Fan Min (1963-), born in Liaoyang, Liaoning.
In 1988 Fan graduated with a Batchelor's Degree from The Faculty of Fine Art of The Jilin Academy of Arts having specialised in printmaking. In 1993 he acted as an assistant in the research class of Printmaking Department of The Central Academy of Fine Arts completing a course of study in the Master's Degree class. Fan graduated with a Master's Degree from The Printmaking Department of The Hong Ik University Research Institute (Korea) in 2001. Fan is currently a Member of the Chinese Printmakers Association, a Deputy-Professor and Head of The Printmaking Department of The Tianjin Academy of Fine Arts.

联系电话 Telephone (86) 13512041063
                                22-6281739
电子信箱 E-mail   mezoofan1@yahoo.com.cn

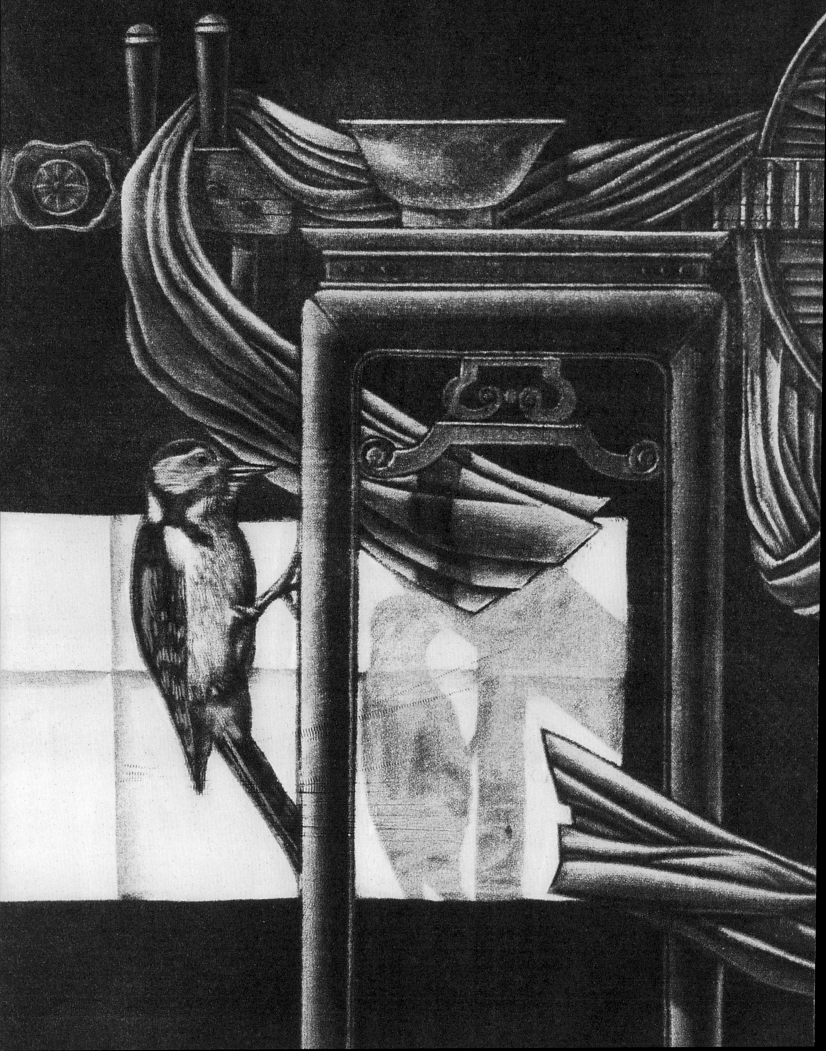

获奖记录

1993 中国西部民族风俗画大展优秀奖

1996 鲁艺杯全国高等师范院校专业教师美术大展银奖

1998 韩国空间国际版画双年展佳作奖

2000 韩国空间国际版画双年展优秀奖

2000 中国青岛国际版画双年展银奖

PRIZES AWARDED

1993 Western China Folk Customs Grand Exhibition, Prize for Outstanding Work

1996 The Lu Xun Academy of Fine Arts Cup in The National Grand Exhibition of The Leading Normal Institutions Specialising in the Teaching of Fine Art, Silver medal

1998 The Space International Print Biennale (Korea), Prize for Excellent Work

2000 The Space International Print Biennale (Korea), Prize for Outstanding Work

2000 The Qingdao International Print Biennale (China), Silver medal

韵——9905　范敏　铜版－美柔汀
Musical sound 9905
Fan Min
Mezzotint
19.5 × 20(cm) 1999

韵——9906 范敏 铜版－美柔汀
Musical sound 9906
Fan Min Mezzotint
29 × 37(cm) 1999

处于一体化、多元化历史发展进程的今天，绘画呈现给观众越来越多的审思。特别是信息技术的巨大能量更直接的刺激着人类的精神情绪。面对这一错综复杂的新格局，绘画一方面实现着自己的艺术主张，一方面创造着个性化分明的画面空间。我在作品《韵》系列中试图通过传统的符号将心中的无形世界转译出来，它不是对传统文化的愉悦向往，而是对传统文化的一种反思，或是一种低吟的伤叹。这或许就是现代人对我们的生存环境形而上的冥想。

ARTIST'S STATEMENT

To be in a body of culture, today's progression of a pluralistic historical development, making art appears to the viewer to need more and more thought. Particularly so is the huge energy of information technology, maybe a direct, perverse stimulation of humankind's spiritual feelings. Confronting this intricate and complex new pattern, making art on one hand fulfils one's own artistic stance and on the other hand it creates an individual pictorial entity. In my work series 'Rhyme' the nature of the imagery, by means of traditional symbols, reveals the invisible world of my heart, it is not a joyful yearning for traditional culture rather a kind of self-examination of traditional culture, or a low chant or injured sigh. The work is perhaps then a contemporary person's metaphysical meditation on our living conditions.

韵——9909 范敏 铜版－美柔汀
Musical sound 9909
Fan Min
Mezzotint
15 × 27.5(cm) 1999

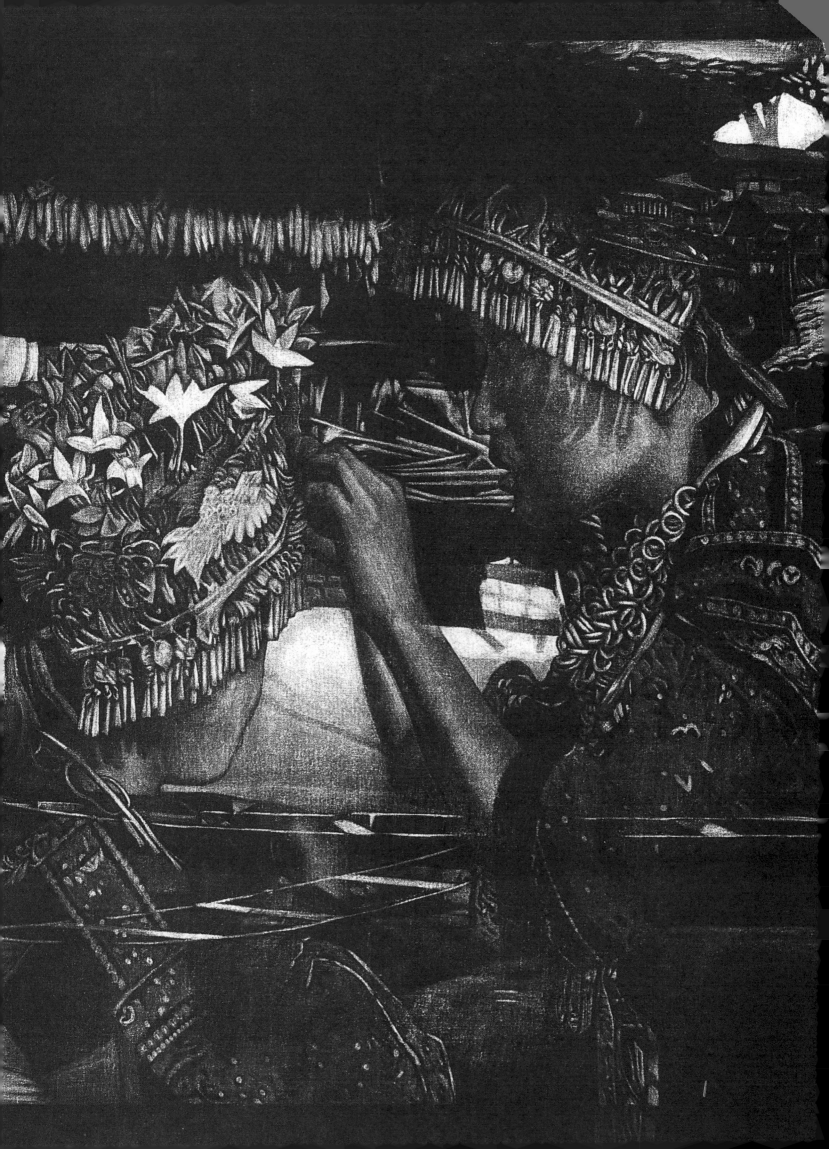

范敏长于铜版画创作，尤精美柔汀技法，其精致的画面，独具的风格为版画语言的拓展开辟了新的空间，成为国内少有的运用此技法进行创作的画家。他结合素材固有的色彩与质感，恰如其分地突显美柔汀的特性，使作品充满了平静、凝重而又神秘的内敛氛围。在精神指向上，蕴含着对传统文化价值的反思，与对当下人类文化、生存境地的思考与批判。

ARTISTIC APPRECIATION

Fan Min is expert in the creation of intaglio prints, particularly so in his use of the technique of mezzotint, its exquisite pictorial qualities, its individual character has opened up a new area for the development of printmaking's language, achieving within China an increase in the creative use of this little used technique among artists. Fan combines the intrinsic colour and character of his source material, for example his accurate display of the specific characteristics of the mezzotint, causing the work to be full of tranquillity, dignity as well as having the mystery of an atmosphere of inner restraint. From the spiritual point of view, the work is accumulating a self-examination of the value of traditional culture and in respect of the culture of contemporary man a reflection and criticism of our living environment.

大地飞歌　范敏　铜版－美柔汀
The fluttering song of the great earth
Fan Min
Mezzotint
37 × 44(cm) 2004

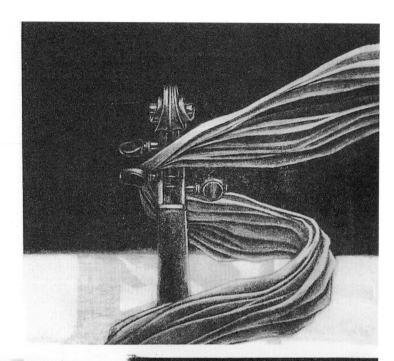

AP.   龍—9901

韵——9807 范敏 铜版－美柔汀
Musical sound 9807
Fan Min
Me zzotint
21 × 24.5(cm) 1999

◄ 韵——9901 范敏 铜版－美柔汀
Musical sound 9901
Fan Min
Mezzotint
26 × 17.5(cm) 1999

韵——9908 范敏 铜版－美柔汀
Musical sound 9908
Fan Min
Mezzotint
24 × 21(cm) 1999

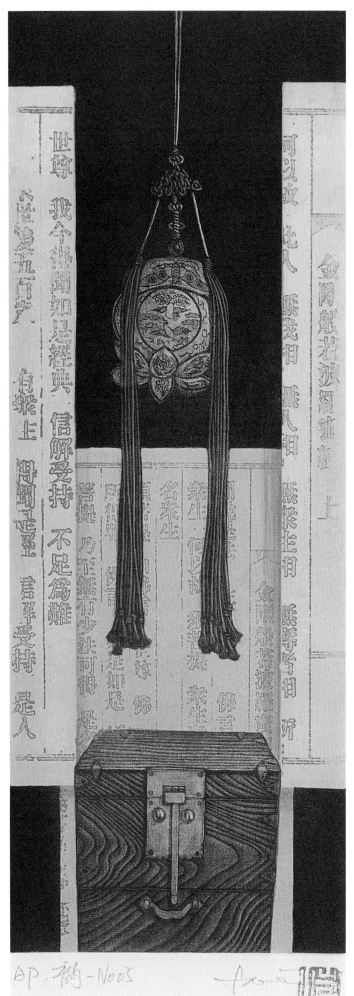

韵——N005　范敏　铜版-美柔汀
Musical sound N005
Fan Min
Mezzotint
27.5 × 10.5(cm)　2000

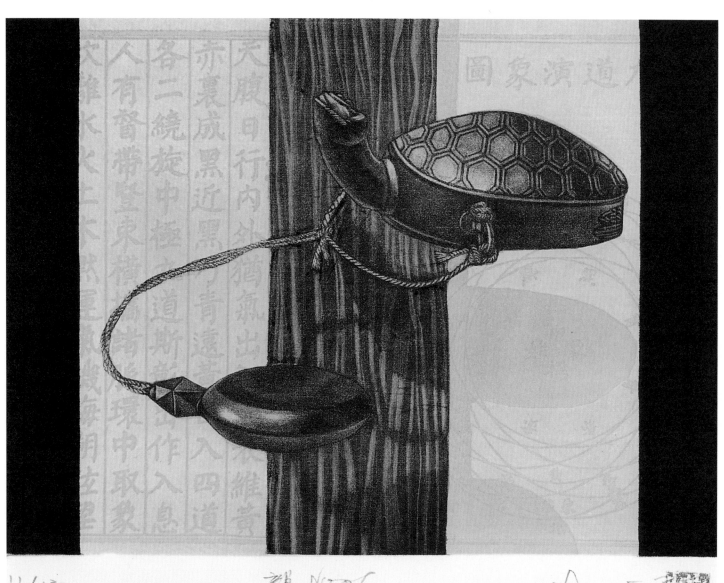

韵—N006　范敏　铜版－美柔汀
Musical sound N006
Fan Min
Mezzotint
16 × 21(cm) 2000

韵—0103　范敏　铜版－美柔汀
Musical sound 0103
Fan Min
Mezzotint
16 × 21(cm)　2001

韵—N101　范敏　铜版－美柔汀
Musical sound N101
Fan Min
Mezzotint
15 × 26(cm)　2001

繁华——近的距离　范敏　铜版－美柔汀
Flowers of different colours---close distance
Fan Min
Mezzotint
20 × 29.5(cm)　2003

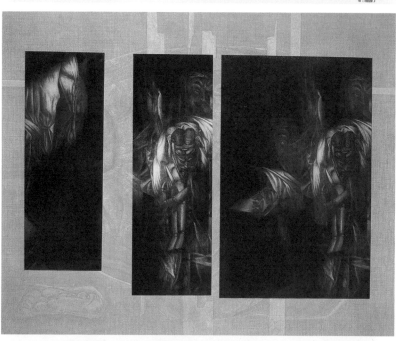

裂—1　范敏　铜版－美柔汀
Split ----I
Fan Min
Mezzotint
40 × 50(cm)　2004

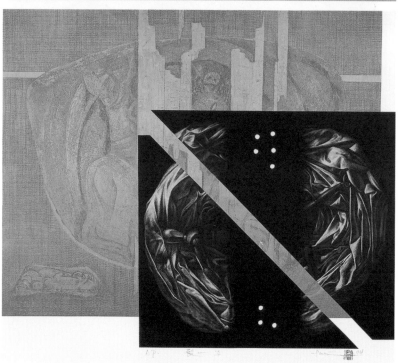

裂—2　范敏　铜版－美柔汀
Split ----II
Fan Min
Mezzotint
43.5 × 52(cm)　2004

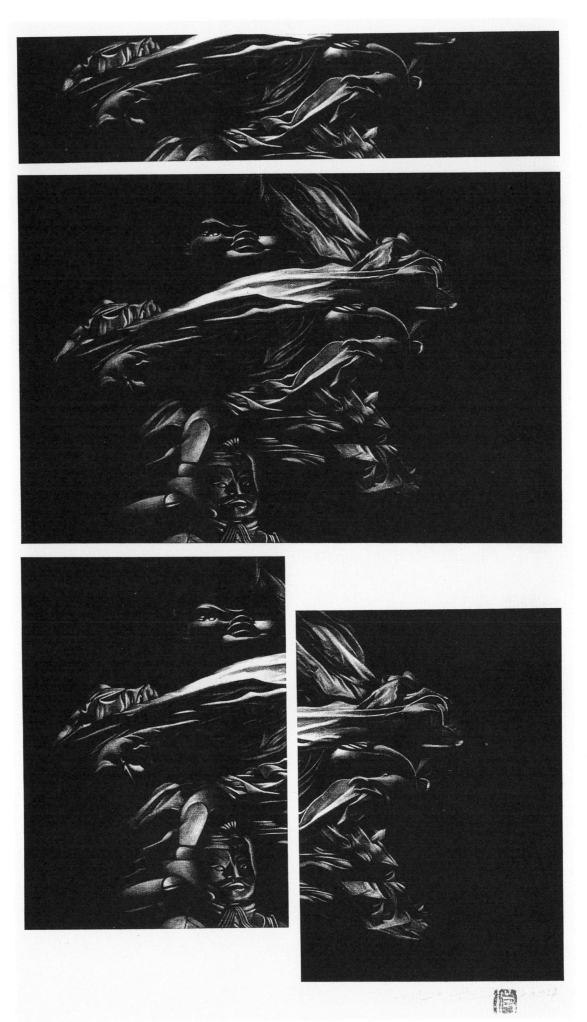

裂—3　范敏　铜版－美柔汀
Split ----III
Fan Min
Mezzotint
50 × 30(cm) 2004

何为民

何为民（1964－　　），黑龙江省牡丹江市人。1982－1986 年就读于哈尔滨师范大学美术系，1988－1991 年，于鲁迅美术学院版画系攻读石版画专业，获硕士学位。1991－1999 年任黑龙江省美术家协会专业画家，自 1997 年，任黑龙江省版画院副秘书长，黑龙江省美术家协会理事，二级美术师，中国美术家协会会员，中国版画家协会会员。1999 年秋至 2005 年，于英国奥斯特大学艺术与设计学院，攻读艺术学硕士及博士学位，现为英国牛津大学东方艺术博士后研究员。

He Weimin (1964-　), born in Mudanjiang, Heilongjiang. He studied in The Faculty of Fine Art of The Harbin Normal University between 1982-1986 and between 1988-1991 he studied Lithography in The Printmaking Department of The Lu Xun Academy of Fine Arts from which he was awarded a Master's degree. He held the position of a Professional Artist in The Heilongjiang Provincial Artist's Association between 1991-1999. From 1997 He also held the post of Deputy-Secretary General of The Heilongjiang Provincial Printmaking Institute and Manager of The Heilongjiang Provincial Artist's Association, he is also a Grade II artist, a Member of The Chinese Artist's Association and a Member of The Chinese Printmaker's Association. Between 1999-2005 He Weimin undertook specialist study in Fine Art at The University of Ulster School of Art and Design where he was awarded a Post-Graduate Diploma (2000) and a Doctorate of Philosophy (2005). He is currently a Post-Doctoral Research Fellow at the Ashmolean Museum, University of Oxford.

联系电话 Telephone (00) 44-7759612577

电子信箱 E-mail　　　hewm.uk@yahoo.com.cn

获奖记录

1990 全国首届青年版画大展铜奖、1992 黑龙江省第五届版画展银奖、1994 全国第十二届版画展铜奖、1996 第三届扎幌国际现代版画双年展评委会奖、全国第六届藏书票展银奖、黑龙江省第六届版画展银奖、庆祝建党七十周年党的生活杯美术作品展铜奖、1999 第九届全国美术大展铜奖、2002 第七届黑龙江省版画展金奖、第十六届全国版画展铜奖。

PRIZES AWARDED

1990 The First National Exhibition of Young Printmakers, Bronze medal

1992 The 5th Heilongjiang Provincial Printmaking Exhibition, Silver medal

1994 The 12th National Printmaking Exhibition, Bronze medal

1996 The 3rd International Contemporary Printmaking Biennale, Selection Committee Prize

1996 The 6th National Exhibition of Ex-Libris, Silver medal

1996 The 6th Heilongjiang Provincial Printmaking Exhibition, Silver medal

1996 The Exhibition of Fine Art to celebrate the 70th anniversary of the founding of the Chinese Communist Party, Life of the Party Cup, Bronze medal

1999 The 9th National Exhibition of Fine Art, Bronze medal

2002 The 7th Heilongjiang Provincial Printmaking Exhibition, Gold medal

2002 The 16th National Printmaking Exhibition, Bronze medal Heilongjiang Fine Art Press, 2000

红灯　何为民　黑白木刻
Red traffic light
He Weimin
Black and white woodcut
49.5 × 60(cm)　1993

老猫　何为民　黑白木刻
Old cat
He Weimin
Black and white woodcut
49.7 × 59.7(cm)　1993

画家心语

艺术需要的不是现代，而是真实，不是表面形式的真实，不是形象的真实，而是情感的与心灵的真实。真实的东西可以久存。

ARTIST'S STATEMENT

The need of art is not for modernity, rather it is reality, not the reality of a superficial form, not the reality of representation rather the reality of emotion, the reality of the heart and of the soul. Those works with reality are able to live forever.

小店　何为民　黑白木刻
Small shop
He Weimin
Black and white woodcut
49.7 × 59.7(cm) 1993

何为民是位学贯中西的高学位的版画家。他本科习油画，研究生三年潜心石版画，所以既有很好的色彩修养，又长于丰富细腻的层次表现，而在黑龙江任专职画家的数年中，又逐渐形成了自己独到的黑白木刻语言。在他的木刻版画中，色彩，光影等因素皆被摈弃，只余下单纯的黑线与白线。话语减少了，涵义的空间却扩充了。黑与白由此更加纯化，且更富有力度。何为民的木刻，初受民间剪纸的启发，继而中国的秦汉瓦当，画像砖及印章等艺术形式也给予他以极其丰厚的养料。对传统道释文化的融会贯通，并以当代语汇重新阐释，使何为民的黑白木刻艺术独步于东西方版画艺坛。

ARTISTIC APPRECIATION

He Weimin is a printmaker who has had the experience of study at a high level in both China and in the West. He first studied oil painting, then as a research student followed a concentrated study of Lithography, therefore having a fine mastery of colour as well as being expert in a rich expression and minute descriptive arrangements of his ideas becoming a professional printmaker in Heilongjiang for several years. He has also gradually formed his own characteristic language for the black and white woodcut. In his woodcut prints colour, shading and other elements have all been abandoned, leaving just simple black lines and white lines. The language has been refined, whilst the space for its meaning has been expanded. Black and white therefore is even purer, even being richer for that strength. He Weimin's woodcut prints were initially inspired by folk paper cuts, then by Qin and Han dynasty eaves tiles, pictorial bricks, seals and other art forms which gave him very rich nourishment. He is well versed in respect of the blending of traditional SDaoist and Buddhist culture and an important new interpretation of it within a contemporary vocabulary, causing He Weimin's black and white woodcuts to be unrivalled within the forum of art in both East and West.

校园欢歌　何为民　黑白木刻
University merry song
He Weimin
Black and white woodcut
41.6 × 38.5(cm)　2001

日子之一　何为民　黑白木刻
Day in day out
He Weimin
Blackand whitewoodcut
59.5 × 50(cm) 1993

公交车　何为民　黑白木刻
The bus
He Weimin
Black and white woodcut
50 × 60(cm) 1994

▶ 都市街头　何为民　黑白木刻
On the street in the capital
He Weimin
Black and white woodcut
59.7 × 50(cm) 1994

II 1/15   In the Street   都市街頭   何山日 Heller 1999

日子之三　何为民　黑白木刻
Diary III
He Weimin
Black and white woodcut
59.7 × 49.7(cm) 1996

日子之四　何为民　黑白木刻
Diary IV
He Weimin
Black and white woodcut
59.7 × 49.7(cm) 1999

三国大将　许褚　何为民　黑白木刻
Three nations Senior General - Xu Chu
He Weimin
Black and white woodcut
29.3 × 22(cm) 2000

沙悟静　何为民　黑白木刻
Stillness of the awakening
He Weimin
Black and white woodcut
29.4 × 22(cm) 2000

北爱日记——公交车 2　何为民　黑白木刻
Northern Ireland diary- bus II
He Weimin
Black and white woodcut
19.5 × 14.2(cm)　2002

18/30　北爱日记-黄昏　何为民　2002

北爱日记——黄昏　何为民　黑白木刻
Northern Ireland diary-dusk
He Weimin
Black and white woodcut
19.5 × 14(cm) 2002

月光 何为民 黑白木刻
Moonlight
He Weimin
Black and white woodcut
19.6 × 14(cm) 2002

校园酒吧　何为民　黑白木刻
University bar
He Weimin
Black and white woodcut
24.5 × 19.8(cm) 2004

李秀

李秀（1943—　），云南石屏人。1968 年毕业于广西艺术学院美术系，师承我国著名画家陈烟桥、阳太阳先生。曾任第四届中国美协理事，第一届全国版画家协会理事，现任云南画院一级美术师。

Li Xiu (1943-　) born in Shiping, Yunnan.

Li graduated from The Department of Fine Art of The Guangxi Academy of Arts in 1968, her teachers having been the nationally famous artists Chen Yanqiao and Yang Taiyang. She has held the posts of Manager of The 4th Exhibition of The Chinese Artist's Association, Manager of The 1st Exhibition of the National Printmakers Association, Li is currently a Grade 1 Artist of The Yunnan Academy of Art.

获奖记录

1982 年作品《啊，马帮！》组画五幅获全国少数民族美展一等奖，1991 年作品《祥云》获第十届全国版画展铜奖，1994 年作品《净水》之一获第八届全国美展优秀奖，1994 年作品《花神》获全国民族百花美展金奖，1997 年作品《塔摆》获全国民族百花美展金奖，1999 年获鲁迅版画奖，2001 年作品《元阳》获第五届全国民族百花美展金奖，2001 年国家民委全国少数民族美术促进会授予"杰出艺术家奖"。

PRIZES AWARDED

1982 The work 'Ah, the caravan', a group of five images, received the 1st Prize at the National Exhibition of Art by the National Minorities

1991 The work 'Auspicious cloud' received the Bronze Medal at the 10th National Exhibition of Printmaking

1994 The work 'Clean water' received the Medal for Outstanding Work at the 8th National Exhibition of Fine Art

1994 The work 'Spirit of flowers' received the Gold Medal at the National Minorities Hundred Flowers Exhibition of Fine Art

1997 The work 'Pagoda arrangement' received the Gold Medal at the National Minorities Hundred Flowers Exhibition of Fine Art

1999 The Lu Xun Printmaking Prize

2001 The work 'The first sun' received the Gold Medal at the 5th National Minorities Hundred Flowers Exhibition of Fine Art

2001 Awarded the title 'Outstanding Fine Artist' by The State Ethnic Affairs Commission, National Minorities Exhibition of Fine Art Promotional Group

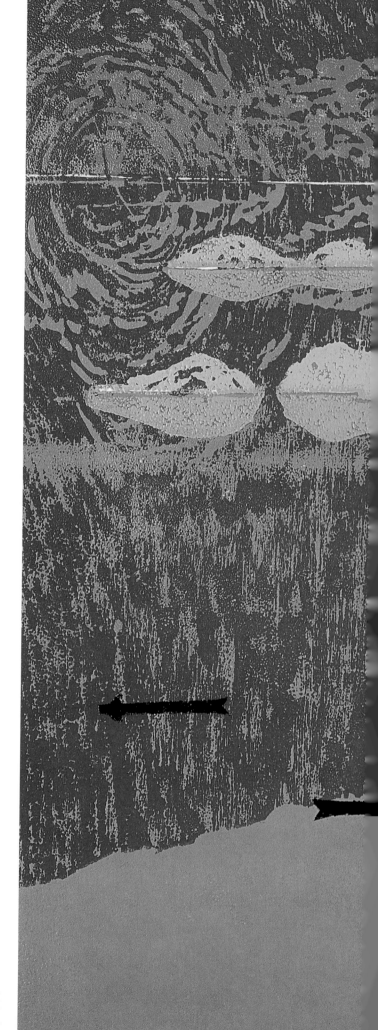

湖光 《啊，马帮》组画之一　李秀　油印套色
Light from the lake　(Ah, the caravan) image series-I
Li Xiu
Multi-colour woodcut printed with oil-based inks
45 × 45(cm)　1982

收藏记录

中国美术馆收藏作品七幅，澳大利亚悉尼美术馆收藏《七月》，
日本森林美术馆收藏作品十四幅，中国驻英国大使馆收藏作品
三幅，神州版画博物馆收藏作品三幅。

出版记录

1996 年出版《李秀版画集》。

WORKS IN THE COLLECTIONS OF

The China Gallery of Fine Art (7 works)

The Sidney Gallery Gallery of Fine Art (the work 'July')

The Shinrin Gallery of Fine Art, Japan (14 works)

The Chinese Embassy, London (3 works)

The Shenzhou Museum of Printmaking (3 works)

PUBLICATIONS

'A collection of works by Li Xiu' 1996

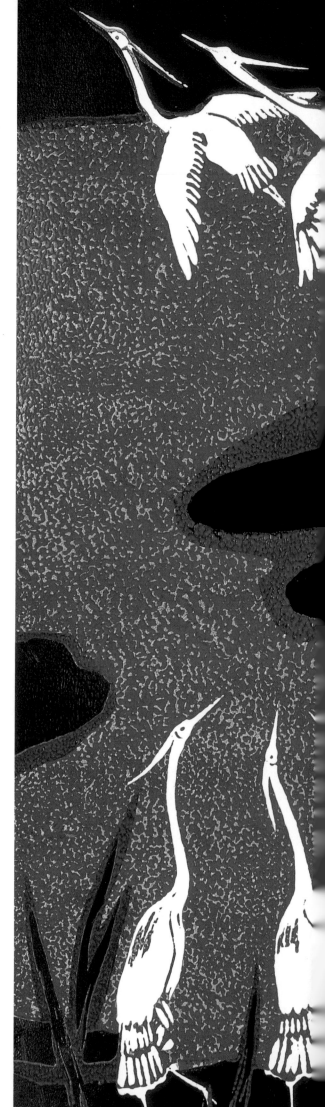

红萍　李秀　油印套色
Red duckweed
Li Xiu
Multi-colour woodcut printed with oil-based inks
42 × 42(cm)　1982

画家心语

个性决定了我在社会角色上的失败，但个性也使我赢得了自我精神满足的空间。

我画山、画水、画……实际上是在画自己。

《雪域组画》的创作，使我无意间走进了自己魂牵梦萦的地方，那里的雪山和湖水高傲而又孤独，我摸索前行，慢慢地远离了尘世的喧嚣，远离了人群，我终于找到了自己的归宿地。

ARTIST'S STATEMENT

My personality has pre-determined the failure that I am in a social role, however, my personality also has won me the space where I feel spiritually satisfied. I have depicted mountains, water, what I have depicted is in fact myself.

Through the creation of the series 'Snowfield', I accidentally entered a dream world and to which I tied my soul; the snow capped mountains and lakes are arrogant and lonely, as I go forward towards this place, I gradually seem far away from the mundane, secular world, seem far away from the crowd, finally I have found a home I belong to.

七月　李秀　油印套色
July
Li Xiu
Multi-colour woodcut printed with oil-based inks
52 × 44.5(cm) 1985

李秀作为我国为数极少的彝族女版画家之一，其作品在题材意蕴与形式语言方面均具有独特性。从艺术学院美术附中到大学阶段接受的严格专业训练使她具有了扎实的功底，云南丰富神奇的大地与少数民族瑰丽多姿的生活为她的创作提供了深厚的滋养。在上世纪七、八十年代，她以女性画家细腻的感受与热情，以具象写实的手法描绘她的彝族兄妹与风物人情。《毕业归来》、《金色的雪山峡谷》、《啊，马帮！》组画等是此期的代表作。1988年《横断山系列》的诞生，标示着李秀的版画创作进入了一个新的阶段，由人物实写转为风景构成，由情感抒发趋向理性的表达，在博大、雄浑、苍凉的意象中，蕴含着一种神秘、沉郁、凝重的原始氛围。这种风格在九十年代的《雪域》、《净水》、《河源》组画中进一步强化，使其作品内蕴着一种深刻的人文内涵与可贵的探索精神。

ARTISTIC EVALUATION

Li Xiu is one of an extremely small number of Yi minority female printmakers, her work has a uniqueness of subject matter and connotation of form and art language. During the period of her attendance at the middle school attached to The Academy of Art and during her time at University Li Xiu received a strict training which gave her a solid foundation in the creation of art. Yunnan's, rich and mystical land and the colourful life of the minority peoples have provided profound and abundant nutrients for her art. During the 1970s to the 1980s, Li Xiu used her delicate female sensitivity and passion in representational techniques portraying her Yi minority brethren and their local conditions and customs. 'Return from the graduation', 'The golden snow mountain and gorge' and the 'Oh, the horse caravan' are the most representative works of this period. The birth of the series 'Hengduan Mountain' in 1988 was a sign that Li Xiu's work had entered a new stage, from when the depiction of representative figures turned into the construction of landscape, from the expression of emotion to rationalistic expression. Among the broad, heroic and desolate psychic images, her work contains a kind of mystic, depressed, dignified and primitive atmosphere. This style was further reinforced in her 1990s series 'Snowfield', 'Pure water' and 'The origin of the river', these works contain kinds of profound humanistic connotations and a valuable spirit of exploration.

起风了 李秀 油印套色
Rising wind
Li Xiu
Multi-colour woodcut printed with oil-based inks
44.5 × 59.5(cm) 1985

悬月《雪城组画》之二　李秀　油印套色
Floating moon (Snowy city image series-II)
Li Xiu
Multi-colour woodcut printed with oil-based inks
60 × 60(cm)　1988

山镜《横断山系列》之三　李秀　油印套色
Mountain mirror (Transverse mountain series-III)
Li Xiu
Multi-colour woodcut printed with oil-based inks
60 × 60(cm)　1988

轮回《雪城组画》之三　李秀　油印套色
Transmigration (Snowy city image series-III)
Li Xiu
Multi-colour woodcut printed with oil-based inks
60 × 60(cm) 1990

紫气 《雪城组画》之四　李秀　油印套色
Purple energy (Snowy city image series-IV)
Li Xiu
Multi-colour woodcut printed with oil-based inks
60 × 60(cm)　1990

祥云 《雪城组画》之一　李秀　油印套色
Auspicious cloud (Snowy city image series-I)
Li Xiu
Multi-colour woodcut printed with oil-based inks
60 × 60(cm)　1990

净水之一 李秀 油印套色
Clean water-I
Li Xiu
Multi-colour woodcut printed with oil-
based inks
55 × 65(cm) 1991

开门节 李秀 油印套色
Open door festival
Li Xiu
Multi-colour woodcut printed with oil-
based inks
55 × 60(cm) 1993

流光 李秀 油印套色
Time
Li Xiu
Multi-colour woodcut printed with oil-based inks
60 × 60(cm) 1993

泉 李秀 油印套色
A spring
Li Xiu
Multi-colour woodcut printed with oil-based inks
60 × 60(cm) 1993

正月 李秀 油印套色
The first month
Li Xiu
Multi-colour woodcut printed with oil-based inks
60 × 60(cm) 1993

元阳 李秀 油印套色
Original sun
Li Xiu
Multi-colour woodcut printed with oil-based inks
50 × 57(cm) 2001

林军

林军（1921—　　），山西平陆县人。1943年初毕业于延安鲁迅文艺学院。曾任晋南军分区编辑、宣传科长、西南军区政治部《西南画报》副主编、中国美术家协会四川分会副主席，现任中国美术家协会会员，四川省美术家协会、神州版画博物馆顾问，国家一级美术师。

Lin Jun (1921-　), born in Pinglu County, Shandong.

In 1943 Lin graduated from The Lu Xun Academy of Literature and Arts in Yan'an. He was assigned as an editor to the south-western military sub-district, a propaganda section chief, a deputy-chief editor for the ' South-western Pictorial' of the south-west military regional government, Deputy –Chairman of The Sichuan branch of The Chinese Artist's Association, presently a member of The Chinese Artist's Association, member of The Sichuan Provincial Artist's Association, a consultant to The Shenzhou Museum of Printmaking and a Grade 1 national artist.

联系电话 Telephone (86) 23-63612988

晋绥军区美术创作一等奖、西南军区美术创作一等奖、首届中国青年美术作品展一等奖，以及全国美术作品展三等奖、优秀奖，四川美术作品展优秀奖、"新兴版画贡献奖"。

PRIZES AWARDED

First prize awarded by the Jinsui military region for artistic creativity

First prize awarded by the south-western military region for artistic creativity

First prize awarded at The First Exhibition of Works by Chinese Youth

Third prize awarded at The National Exhibition of Fine Art

A prize for outstanding merit

A prize for outstanding merit awarded at The Sichuan Exhibition of Fine Art

The ' Prize for a Contribution to the New Printmaking'

追捕　林军　木刻
Pursue and capture
Lin Jun
Woodcut
22 × 17.5(cm) 1951

出版记录
连环木刻《不朽的战士》、《剿匪英雄李殿增》、《林军木刻选集》等。

收藏记录
中国美术馆、大英博物馆、欧洲木版基金会、神州版画博物馆、江苏美术馆、广东美术馆、山西省博物馆、天津市博物馆、辽宁省博物馆、挪威比勒国际版画展览中心、欧洲世界金融基金会等收藏二百余幅。

PUBLICATIONS

The picture-story books ' The Immortal Soldier', 'The brave Li Dianzeng, suppressor of bandits' and ' A selection of woodcut prints by Lin Jun' among others.

WORKS IN THE COLLECTIONS OF

The China Gallery of Fine Art

The British Museum

The Muban Foundation

The Shenzhou Museum of Printmaking

The Jiangsu Gallery of Fine Art

The Guangdong Gallery of Fine Art

The Shanxi Provincial Museum

The Tianjin City Museum

The Liaoning Provincial Museum

The Norwegian International E x hibition Centre, Bergen

The European World Banking Foundation

These and other collections contain more than 200 of the artist's works.

喊话劝降　林军　木刻
Propaganda to surrender
Lin Jun
Woodcut
18 × 23(cm) 1951

外国游客、画友常问我：你是否到过外国？我说：中国幅员辽阔、丰富多彩，我一辈子、十辈子都画不完、用不尽，所以从没有出国门的打算。这是我的真心话，我认为：每个画家都是根据自己的生活经历，思想观点来进行艺术实践的，很难面面周到。

ARTIST'S STATEMENT

Foreign guests and artist friends often ask me ' Have you ever travelled abroad' ? I say ' China is a vast territory, it is rich in colourful life, in my lifetime, even in ten lifetimes I could not finish painting it, I have more than enough to do, therefore I have never reckoned on going beyond the gates of China. I say this very sincerely, I consider, every artist creates their work based on their own experience of life, their thoughts and ideas should enter into their artistic practice, it is very difficult to be attentive to every aspect.

挑刺　林军　木刻
Finding fault
Lin Jun
Woodcut
41 × 52.5(cm) 1988

艺术评介

林军是位已有60余年创作生涯的老版画家，是一位讴歌人民，紧随时代、富有社会责任感，淳朴、勤奋，具有农民气质的艺术家。抗日战争时期便创作了一批木刻肖像和连环木刻，其中《不朽的战士》以多变的构图、巧妙的黑白处理，与生动的人物塑造而受到好评。建国后以苗族生活、西南风光与革命历史题材创作的《苗岭山麓》、《巫峡》等一批版画风格细腻，刀法缜密，具有较高的艺术价值。上世纪70年代末至80年代初，是他版画创作的一个新高峰，《清江归牧》、《憩睡的峡谷》、《峡江幽邃图》等多幅作品参加全国及省级展览，频频获奖并被美术馆收藏。林军人物与风景版画兼长，人物刻划造型生动，风景版画以层次丰富的灰色调展现宏阔的构图与庞大的气势，以一丝不苟的创作态度与朴茂的画风，表现大自然的壮美，与画家对祖国河山的一片深情。

ARTISTIC EVALUATION

Lin Jun is an individual with a creative career as a printmaker stretching over more than 60 years, he is a person celebrated in song, closely following the times, having full feelings of social responsibility, honest, diligent, an artist having a peasant's temperament During the period of the anti-Japanese war he created a series of woodcut portraits and picture-books, among which were ' The immortal soldier ' with many varied compositions, an ingenious handling of black and white with vivid figure modelling and receiving favourable comment.

After Liberation, through the life of the Miao nationality, the grandeur of the south-west and revolutionary history material he created ' At the foot of Mt. Miao ', ' The Wu gorge ', and other series of prints in a fine style, his cutting methods are meticulous, having a comparatively high artistic value. The work of late 1970s and the early 1980s represented a new peak in his creative printmaking, 'Returning from herding along the Qing river', ' The sleeping gorge ', ' The river and gorge, deep and tranquil ' and many other works were included in national and provincial e x hibitions, repeatedly being awarded prizes and being added to the collections of galleries of fine art. Lin Jun is e x pert in making prints of both figures and landscape, his figures cut with lively modelling, the prints of landscape in rich arrangements of grey e x press e x pansive compositions and imposing manner, with a scrupulous and meticulous creative approach, Lin creates a great natural majesty, an artist with deep feelings of love towards the rivers and mountains of his homeland.

生命啊！常青　林军　木刻
Life, Ah. Evergreen
Lin Jun
Woodcut
57 × 41(cm) 1995

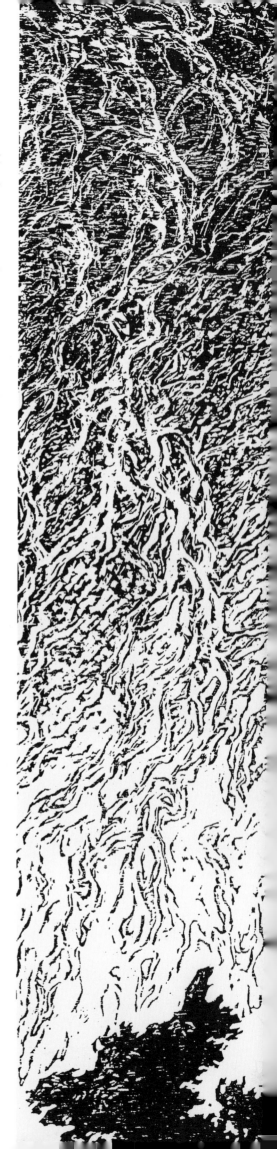

衷心的欢迎 (木刻)

林军 1951年作

衷心的欢迎　林军　木刻
Heartfelt welcome
Lin Jun
Woodcut
30 × 16(cm) 1951

▶放学归途　林军　木刻
Homeward journey after
school
Lin Jun
Woodcut
45.5 × 29.5(cm) 1953

9/50　放学归途（木刻）　北京 中国美术馆 收藏　伦敦 大英博物馆 收藏　林军 1953年作于重庆

冲锋号　林军　木刻
A bugle call to charge
Lin Jun
Woodcut
94 × 40.5(cm) 1957

艰苦岁月　林军　木刻
Difficult years
Lin Jun
Woodcut
82 × 116(cm)　1957

志愿军二级战斗英雄黄丑和
林军　木刻
Volunteer Warrant Officer, the
heroic Huang Chouhe
Lin Jun
Woodcut
48 × 38.5(cm)　1962

追歼　林军　木刻
Pursue and destroy
Lin Jun
Woodcut
46 × 35(cm)　1972

出击　林军　木刻
Launching an attack
Lin Jun
Woodcut
46 × 35 (cm)　1972

为独立为解放 林军 木刻
For individual liberation
Lin Jun
Woodcut
58 × 80(cm) 1981

八路女杰陈少敏 林军 木刻
Eighth Route Army heroin Chen Shaomin
Lin Jun
Woodcut
32 × 22(cm) 1993

牛文

牛文（1922—　），山西灵石人。1943 年毕业于延安鲁迅文艺学院美术系。曾任晋绥边区美术家协会秘书长。建国后历任中国美术家协会理事、中国版画家协会副主席、四川美术家协会主席等职。现任中国版画家协会顾问，四川省美术家协会名誉主席。

Niu Wen (1922 -　), born in Lingshi, Shanxi.
In 1943 Niu graduated from The Faculty of Fine Art in The Lu xun Academy of Literature and Arts in Yan'an. He was assigned to act as the Secretary-General of The Shanxi-Hebei Border Area Artist's Association. After the founding of new China, Niu successively held the posts of Member of the Executive Council of The Chinese Artist's Association, Deputy-Chair of The Chinese Printmaker's Association and the Chair of The Sichuan Artist's Association among other administrative posts. He is currently acting as a consultant to The Chinese Printmaker's Association and the Honorary Chair of The Sichuan Provincial Artist's Association.

联系电话 Telephone (86) 28-87427288

分别在第六、七届全国美展、全国版展、全国少数民族美展及日本获奖,1991 年获中国美术家协会、中国版画家协会颁发的"新兴版画杰出贡献奖"。

PRIZES AWARDED

Niu has been respectively awarded prizes at The 6th and 7th National Exhibition of Fine Art, The National Exhibition of Printmaking, The National Exhibition of Fine Art from the National Minorities and a prize from Japan. In 1991 he was awarded a prize from The Chinese Artist's Association and the prize for 'An Outstanding Contribution to New Printmaking' awarded by the Chinese Printmakers Association.

听胜利消息　牛文　木刻
Listening to the victory news
Niu Wen
Woodcut
14.2 × 18(cm)　1949

收藏记录

60 余幅作品被中国美术馆、辽宁省博物馆、天津市博物馆、大英博物馆、欧洲木版基金会等收藏。

出版记录

《牛文作品集》、《牛文版画选集》、《雪山红日》等。

WORKS IN THE COLLECTIONS OF

More than 60 Works In The Collections of:

The China Gallery of Fine Art

The Liaoning Provincial Museum

The Tianjin City Museum

The British Museum

The Muban Foundation

PUBLICATIONS

A collection of works by Niu Wen

A selection of prints by Niu Wen

Snowy mountain and red sun, among other works.

军属给前方写信　牛文　木刻
The soldier's family send a letter to the Front
Niu Wen
Woodcut
18.4 × 27.3(cm) 1949

吉祥如意遍地锦　牛文　木刻
A brocade covered with auspicious and good wishes
Niu Wen
Woodcut
31 × 46(cm) 1959

牛文是我国人物版画的代表画家之一，也是四川版画的领导者、组织者。他建国前创作的《领回土地证》、《丈地》等一批反映解放区生活的作品浑厚朴实，具有丰厚、沉重的社会历史内容。建国后他多次深入藏区，成为藏民生活执着的雕刻者。1959 年《吉祥如意遍地锦》、《欢乐的藏族儿童》两幅作品的推出，标志着牛文艺术的成熟与追求的转变，一改过去的繁富拘谨而为粗放流畅、简洁有力，由叙事趋向抒情，更重作品的审美价值。牛文版画大的突破，形成明显的艺术个性是在改革开放的新时期。此时，他从古代徽派版画及民间皮影、剪纸、传统戏曲的脸谱服饰中汲取营养，以比国画白描还精细的效果表现线的韵律美。《草地新征》、《朝阳》、《赛马图》等，以朴茂、含蓄的东方情韵与单纯、强烈的现代构成相融合，既有大块黑白的对比，又有线刻精细清秀的韵致，其深邃清新的意境与优雅别致的装饰效果体现出画家独特鲜明的个性。

ARTISTIC EVALUATION

Niu Wen is a primary figure in the representation of Chinese printmakers, he is also a leader and organizer of printmaking in Sichuan province. The works 'Receiving back the land certificate', and 'Marking out the land' and others series created before the establishment of new China reflected life in the liberated areas, they are bold and vigorous, carrying a rich and heavy socio-historical content. After Liberation he went many times to the region of Tibet, becoming a woodcut artist dedicated to depicting the Tibetan's life. In 1959 his works 'A brocade covered with auspicious and good wishes' and 'Happy Tibetan children' were presented, indicating changes in Niu Wen's artistic maturity and direction, a changing of goals with the complicated richness and over-caution being replaced by a tendency towards narration in a simple, forceful, bold and fluent expression of emotions stressing the aesthetic value of the works. The great breakthrough in Niu Wen's prints took the form of a distinct artistic individuality and happened during the new period of the open door policy. At that time, he absorbed nutrition from the antique prints of the Hue school, folk donkey-skin shadow theatre, paper cuts and traditional operatic facial make-up and costumes, expressing the beauty of rhythmic linearity, an effect contrasting with the clarity and finesse of lines drawn with brush and ink in national painting. 'A new campaign on the grasslands', 'The morning sun' and 'Horse racing' were simple, straightforward, an embodiment of oriental rhythms and simplicity mixed with a strong, contemporary composition, with large areas of contrast in black and white, also having lines cut with a fine and delicate elegance, the profound purity and freshness of mood with the graceful, unconventional decorative effects reveal the artist's unique and distinct individuality.

朝阳　牛文　木刻
The morning sun
Niu Wen
Woodcut
56 × 96(cm) 1984

丈地（木刻）12/50 1949 牛文

丈地 牛文　木刻
Marking out the land
Niu Wen
Woodcut
18.5 × 29(cm)　1949

雅鲁赞布江畔 牛文　套色木刻
Beside the Yalu Tsangpo river
Niu Wen
Woodcut
9.5 × 25(cm)　1956

康藏道旁　牛文　木刻
Beside the Kang Tibet road
Niu Wen
Woodcut
23.2 × 46(cm) 1956

村头　牛文　木刻
The edge of the village
Niu Wen
Woodcut
14 × 23(cm) 1956

东方红、太阳升（木刻）
1/50 1959年 牛文

欢乐的藏族儿童 牛文 木刻
Happy Tibetan children
Niu Wen
Woodcut
32 × 30.5(cm) 1959

为包拯造像　牛文　木刻
A portrait for Bao Zheng
Niu Wen
Woodcut
46.5 × 31.8(cm)　1980

萧何月下追韩信　牛文　木刻
Xiao He pursuing Han Xin under the moon
Niu Wen
Woodcut
70 × 49(cm)　1984

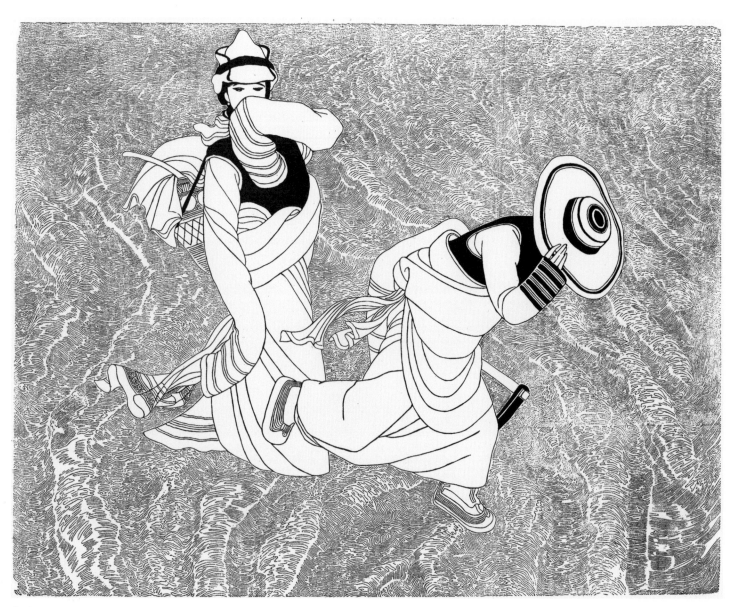

春雷　牛文　木刻
Spring thunder
Niu Wen
Woodcut
54.7 × 69.6(cm)　1984

▶　赛马图　牛文　木刻
Horse racing
Niu Wen
Woodcut
96.8 × 66.3(cm)　1985

赛马图（木刻）1985 45/50 牧文

新路 牛文　木刻
The new road
Niu Wen
Woodcut
83 × 56.5(cm)　1987

中国戏剧人物——项羽 牛文　木刻
Chinese theatrical characters – Xiang Yu
Niu Wen
Woodcut
13.5 × 10.5(cm)　1988

中国戏剧人物——苏武 牛文　木刻
Chinese theatrical characters – Su Wu
Niu Wen
Woodcut
13.5 × 10.5(cm)　1988

中国戏剧人物——钟馗 牛文　木刻
Chinese theatrical characters – Zhong Kui
Niu Wen
Woodcut
13.5 × 10.5(cm)　1988

其加达瓦

其加达瓦 (1946–   )，四川甘孜人、藏族。1964年毕业于四川美术学院，曾任四川省美术家协会秘书长、常务副主席，四川美术馆副馆长。现任深圳画院常务副院长、深圳市文联、美协副主席、中国美术家协会理事、中国美术家协会版画艺术委员会委员等职。

Qijia Dawa (1946-), born in Ganzi, Sichuan, of the Tibetan minority people. Qijia graduated from The Sichuan Academy of Fine Arts, becoming appointed as Secretary-General to The Sichuan Provincial Artist's Association, Deputy-Chair of Association Business, Deputy-Director of The Sichuan Gallery of Fine Art. Qijia currently holds the posts of the Executive Deputy-Director for The Shenzhen Art Academy, Shenzhen City Cultural Federation, Deputy-Chair of the Fine Art Association, Manager of The Chinese Artist's Association, Member of The Chinese Artist's Association Printmaking Committee among others.

联系电话 Telephone (86) 755-83982992

1982 年全国首届少数民族美术作品展览佳作奖、首届中国少数民族美术作品展铜奖、第二届中国少数民族美展银奖、1987年中国现代版画展金奖（日本）、1994 年第八届全国美展优秀作品奖。1993 年获国务院颁发的政府特殊津贴。1999 年获"鲁迅版画奖"、四川省文联授予的"德艺双馨艺术家"称号、2001 年获中国美协、中国少数民族美术促进会授予的"民族杰出艺术家"称号。

PRIZES AWARDED

1982 The Inaugural Exhibition of Art from the National Minorities, Prize for Excellent Work

Bronze medal, The Inaugural Exhibition of Art from the Chinese Minority Peoples

Silver Medal, The 2nd Exhibition of Art from the Chinese Minority Peoples

1987 Gold Medal, Chinese Contemporary Prints Exhibition, Japan

1993 Awarded a Government Special Stipend promulgated by the Chinese State Council

1994 The 8th National Exhibition of Fine Art, Prize for Outstanding Work

1999 Awarded the Lu xun Printmaking Prize

1999 Awarded the title 'Dual Qualities of Moral and Artistic', Sichuan Provincial Cultural Federation

2001 Awarded the title 'Outstanding National Minority Artist', the Chinese Artist's Association Chinese Minorities Promotion Group

密林中　其加达瓦　黑白木刻
In the dense wood
Qijia Dawa
Black and white woodcut
41 × 54(cm)　1979

WORKS IN THE COLLECTION OF

The China Gallery of Fine Art

The Beijing Minority People's Cultural Palace

The Liaoning Provincial Museum

The Shenzhou Museum of Printmaking

The Shenzhen Gallery of Fine Art

The Muban Foundation, London

Among others, more than 30 works are in the collections of institutions both inside China and overseas.

PUBLICATIONS

'A selection of works by Qijia Dawa'

寻医路上　其加达瓦　黑白木刻
On the road looking for a Doctor
Qijia Dawa
Black and white woodcut
37 × 40(cm) 1980

画家心语

川藏公路是藏区历史巨变的见证，我的命运和事业也和她相伴而行。40年前，是她第一次送我踏上了四川美术学院的艺术殿堂。记得，我创作的第一幅版画作品《开路》就是以这条公路为题材，描绘军民情深的动人场面。几十年来，我一次又一次地通过她来到故乡和藏族人民的怀抱，亲身体验人民的酸甜苦辣，深切感受雪山高原和人民生活发生着的历史巨变。当我们坐在帐篷里喝着香喷喷的酥油茶、当我们在草地上跳起欢乐的弦子锅庄，当我们共同扬起青稞，同享丰收的喜悦时，雪山高原的博大、宏伟、人民的善良、勤劳深深地振动我的心，抑制不住的创作欲望和冲动使我一次次拿起画笔与刻刀，一幅幅版画作品像清泉从我心里流出。这些作品是我真实情感的流露，是我审美理想的追求，他们饱含着我的欢乐与痛苦。我，一个童年时衣不蔽体的孤儿，能从事高尚的艺术事业几十年，并且艺术成果能得到社会各方的承认和肯定，我从心里感到由衷的喜悦和幸福。

ARTIST'S STATEMENT

The road between Sichuan and Tibet is witness to the huge changes that have occurred in the history of the Tibetan region, my own destiny and enterprise have also followed it. Forty years ago it was this road that delivered me to the palace of The Sichuan Academy of Fine Art. I remember, that this road became the subject matter of my first print ' Blazing a trail ', it depicts a touching scene of soldiers and ordinary citizens. A few decades later, I was time and again travelling along this road to my hometown to embrace Tibetan people, to experience the people's joys and sorrows.I was deeply moved by the high plains of the snowy mountains and the huge historical changes in the lives of the people. When we were sitting in tents drinking the sweet tasting butter tea, when we were dancing on the grassy earth to the cheerful folk dance of the sanxian lute, when we were together winnowing the highland barley, sharing the joy of the bumper harvest, the breadth of the high plains of the snowy mountains, the grandeur, the people's kind-heartedness, their diligence deeply shook my heart, I could not restrain my creative urge and impulse to time after time pick up my brush and my wood cut knife, print after print seemed to flow from my heart like a clear stream. These works betray my true emotions, they are the pursuit of my aesthetic ideals, they encapsulate my joys and my sorrows. As for me, in my childhood I was a boy in shabby clothes, now I am engaged in this noble artistic pursuit for several decades, moreover my artistic achievement has been acknowledged and affirmed from every aspect of society, from the bottom of my heart I feel sincere happiness and joy.

帐篷里的歌　其加达瓦　黑白木刻
A song in the tent
Qijia Dawa
Black and white woodcut
39 × 49(cm) 1980

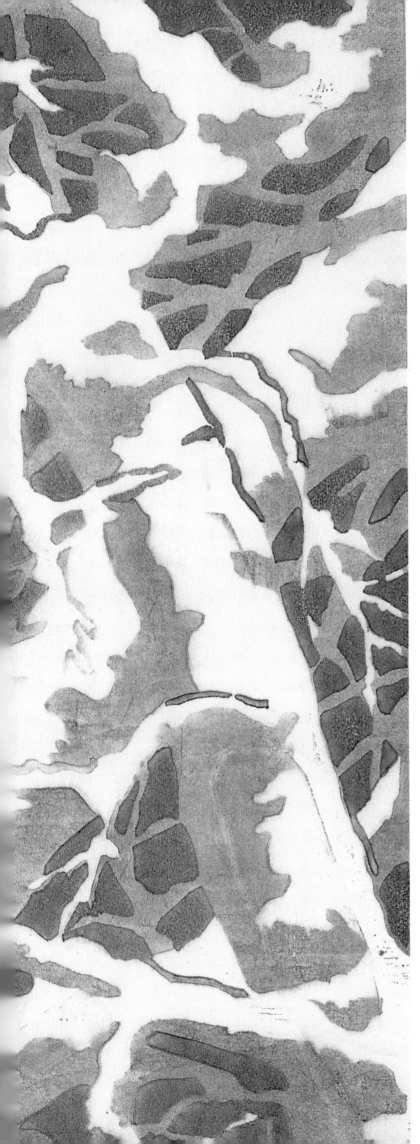

其加达瓦是我国杰出的藏族版画家。他以对新旧生活的切身体验，对自己民族的深刻理解，真实地反映藏民的苦与乐，热情地讴歌藏民的新生活。他 14 岁考入四川美术学院民族班，19 岁以优异成绩毕业被选进四川省美术家协会，成为专业画家，当年创作的《开路》，起步便高，在《人民日报》上发表，产生很大影响。"文革"后其创作形成高峰，风格逐渐显露。他以刻划黑白人物见长，兼攻水印与油印套色版画。《瑞雪》、《密林中》、《金色的秋天》、《育林人》等均具代表性。其加达瓦刻苦、勤奋，创作态度极其认真，制作一丝不苟，他的版画大都构图饱满，黑白对比强烈，人物精雕细刻，性格开朗粗放，具有一种力量感和阳刚之美。

ARTISTIC EVALUATION

Qijia Dawa is China's outstanding printmaker of Tibetan nationality. By reference to recent and past experiences of life and through a deep understanding of his own people, he can truly reflect the joys and sorrows of the Tibetans, warmly celebrating in song the new life of the Tibetan people. At fourteen years of age, Qijia passed the entrance examination to enter The Sichuan Academy of Fine Arts, at nineteen he graduated with outstanding success, being selected to join The Sichuan Provincial Artist's Association becoming a professional printmaker. In the same year his work began to be recognised, the print 'Blazing the trail' being published in 'The People's Daily', which exercised a wide influence. Following the 'Cultural Revolution' his work reached its peak of achievement, his style gradually revealing itself. Qijia is a master in the cutting of black and white portraits, also for his skill in the making of multi-block prints printed with both water-soluble colours and oil-based inks. His works 'Auspicious snow', 'In the dense wood', 'An Autumn sky, the colour of gold', 'A planter of trees' and other works have representative qualities. Qijia Dawa is assiduous, industrious, bringing a high degree of understanding to his work, the majority of his prints are richly composed, with strong black and white contrasts, the portraits are finely cut, their nature open and clear, having a kind of strength of feeling and a virile beauty.

瑞雪　其加达瓦　水印木刻
Auspicious snow
Qijia Dawa
Black and white woodcut
48 × 45(cm)　1980

18/50　远方来客　　　　　　　　　　　　　　　　其加达瓦　1979年

远方来客　其加达瓦　黑白木刻
A guest from afar
Qijia Dawa
Black and white woodcut
38 × 43(cm)　1979

远牧 其加达瓦　油印套色木刻
Distant herding
Qijia Dawa
Multi-colour woodcut printed　with oil-based colours
32 × 48(cm) 1980

踏破高原雪 其加达瓦　油印套色木刻
Old temple on the high pastures
Qijia Dawa
Multi-colour woodcut printed　with oil-based colours
35 × 44.5(cm) 1980

牧笛 其加达瓦　黑白木刻
Herding flute
Qijia Dawa
Black and white woodcut
40 × 47(cm) 1982

雪山花　其加达瓦　黑白木刻
Snowy mountain flower
Qijia Dawa
Black and white woodcut
49 × 54(cm) 1982

育林人 其加达瓦　黑白木刻
The forestry man
Qijia Dawa
Black and white woodcut
67 × 90(cm) 1984

33/100　　金色的秋天　　　　　　　　　　　　　贾加慕画（藏族）1984年

14/50　　　心愿　　　其加达瓦 1957年作

心愿　其加达瓦　黑白木刻
Cherished hope
Qijia Dawa
Black and white woodcut
53 × 46(cm) 1987

◀ **金色的秋天**　其加达瓦　黑白木刻
Golden autumnal sky
Qijia Dawa
Black and white woodcut
80 × 72(cm) 1984

24/100 —沉思   其加达瓦 1994年

◀ **沉思** 其加达瓦 黑白木刻
Meditation
Qijia Dawa
Black and white woodcut
67 × 53(cm) 1994

驰骋 其加达瓦 黑白木刻
Gallop
Qijia Dawa
Black and white woodcut
80 × 65(cm) 2001

母与子 其加达瓦 黑白木刻
Mother and child
Qijia Dawa
Black and white woodcut
78 × 55(cm) 2003

宋源文

宋源文（1933—　），辽宁大连人。中央美术学院版画系毕业后留校，曾任版画系主任、教授。先后担任中国版画家协会秘书长、常务副主席、1999 年开始任中国美术家协会版画艺术委员会主任。

Song Yuanwen (1933-), born in Dalian, Liaoning.

After graduating from The Central Academy of Fine Arts, Song remained at the Academy to teach, eventually being appointed to the post of Head of The Printmaking Department and Professor. Song successively held the posts of Secretary-General of The Chinese Printmaker's Association, Deputy-Chair of Party Affairs and in 1999 he began the appointment of Head of The Chinese Artist's Association Printmaking Committee.

联系电话 Telephone　(86) 10-64713964

获奖记录

1986 年英国第九届大不列颠国际版画双年展获奖。

PRIZES AWARDED

The Ninth Bradford International Print Biennale Prize,
1986

不眠的大地　宋源文　黑白木刻
The unsleeping earth
Song Yuanwen
Black and white woodcut
43 × 80(cm) 1979

WORKS IN THE COLLECTIONS OF

The China Gallery of Fine Art

The Gallery of the Central Academy of Fine Arts

The Yan Huang Museum of Arts, Beijing

The Lu xun Museum, Beijing

The Beijing City Artist's Association

The Shenzhou Museum of Printmaking

The Liaoning Provincial Museum

The Shenzhen Gallery of Fine Art

The British Museum

The Lutheran Museum, Germany among others.

PUBLICATIONS

Song has published more than 50 articles on Fine Art practice.

疾风劲柳　　宋源文　　黑白木刻
The strong wind and the sturdy willows
Song Yuanwen
Black and white woodcut
34 × 56.5(cm) 1980

画家心语

我偏爱自然风光，那丰富的视觉形象资源，千姿百态，风情万种；我更爱北国风光，那独特的地域特色，沧桑世寰，人文精神铸就了我宣泄内心情感的文化平台。依我个人的体悟，积生活中的万千感受，几乎都可以在自然界中找到呼应。从自然生活中反映社会生活，不仅可以展示视觉形象之审美享受，亦可以从另一个视角引发对于社会内涵的反思，达到寓情于景、情景交融的艺术境界。诗情画意，是中国传统美学思想所崇尚的艺术境界。至今我仍然认为它是笃信为人生而艺术的高尚境界。

ARTIST'S STATEMENT

I prefer natural scenery, preferring that natural resource of rich visual imagery, thousands of impressions in hundreds of poses, tens of thousands of different feelings; I am particularly fond of the landscape of northern China, those districts with their distinctive character, those that have experienced a tough history, forging the spirit of humanism which gave me a cultural platform to give vent to my innermost feelings. Depending on my individual self-enlightenment and the myriad experiences of life, as if all can be found reflected within nature. From within a natural life one may reflect the life of society, one can not only present the enjoyment of visual images, but one can also bring introspection to the connotations of society from a different perspective, achieving a state of grafting emotion onto landscape, mingling artistic boundaries. Qualities suggestive of poetry and painting are China's traditional aesthetic in the upholding of artistic boundaries. Even today I still consider that poetic sentiment and pictorial means is genuinely a lofty boundary in creating art for the purpose of life.

月明松清　宋源文　黑白木刻
The bright moon, the green pines
Song Yuanwen
Black and white woodcut
31 × 53(cm) 1981

艺术评介

宋源文是当今中国版画界的主要领导人与重大版画活动的策划、组织者，他在此方面倾注了大量的精力，对中国版画的发展起到了引导与推动作用。原来曾担任中央美术学院版画系主任，在版画教育、人才培养方面亦有较大贡献。他的版画创作以黑白风景为主，《疾风劲柳》、《不眠的大地》、《长空行》、《野花盛开的地方》等以开阔的构图，抒情的笔调，展现北国景观豪放的气势、神奇的魅力与壮观的物象。他的木刻版画以抒情见长，以气势取胜，往往在自然景物的描绘中蕴含某种社会内容，漾溢着某种诗情画意，表现某种人文精神，使人们在审美观照中受到情绪的感染，获取奋进的力量。在艺术表现上或线刻，或点刻，刀法单纯，但层次丰富，画面整体但动感强烈，在动与静，繁与简，明与暗的效果对比中，呈现出引人入胜的境地。

ARTISTIC EVALUATION

Song Yuanwen is an important leader in the field of Chinese printmaking and a major planner and organizer of important printmaking events, he has devoted enormous energy in guiding the upward development of Chinese printmaking and pushing forward its usage. Song Yuanwen was originally appointed The Head of The Printmaking Department of The Central Academy of Fine Arts, working in printmaking education, training and cultivating talent, he has made a larger than usual contribution. His creativity is primarily in black and white woodcut prints of landscape, examples being 'The forceful wind tests the strength of the willow', 'The vast and sleepless land', 'Crossing the immense sky', 'The place where wild flowers bloom' and others, with an open composition and expressive style the bold and unrestrained landscape of the northern scenery emerges before our eyes with mystical enchantment and grand appearance. His woodcut prints with an expertise at expressing ideas, with success in their imposing manner, more often than not contain various kinds of social content within their drawing of natural scenery natural, brimming with a variety of poetic feelings and pictorial means, expressing different aspects of the human spirit, enabling people through the appreciation of beauty to experience emotional effects, to gain power in their progress. In artistic expression or in the cutting of lines or of dots, Song's cutting techniques are simple and pure, yet his arrangement of ideas is rich. The picture surface has an integrity yet an active strength, in movement and stillness, manifold yet selective, in their contrasting effects of brightness and darkness, the prints present an enchanting scene.

晨光　宋源文　黑白木刻
Morning light
Song Yuanwen
Black and white woodcut
46 × 73(cm)　2003

黑龙江初雪　宋源文　黑白木刻
Early snow in Heilongjiang
Song Yuanwen
Black and white woodcut
32.6 × 64(cm)　1980.10

雁鸣长空　宋源文　黑白木刻
The cry of the wild geese in the vast sky
Song Yuanwen
Black and white woodcut
41 × 71(cm)　1984

廻旋曲　宋源文　黑白木刻
Rondo
Song Yuanwen
Black and white woodcut
43 × 67(cm)　1989

柳烟梦　宋源文　黑白木刻
Dreaming of the misty willows
Song Yuanwen
Black and white woodcut
46 × 66(cm)　1990

长空万点觅归巢　宋源文　黑白木刻

In a vast sky ten thousand dots seeking a return to the nest

Song Yuanwen

Black and white woodcut

45 × 71(cm)　1991

野花盛开的地方 宋源文 黑白木刻
Where the wild flowers bloom
Song Yuanwen
Black and white woodcut
46 × 85.5(cm) 1992

长空行 宋源文 黑白木刻
Crossing the vast sky
Song Yuanwen
Black and white woodcut
43 × 80(cm) 1994

渡过寒冬　宋源文　黑白木刻
To tide over the severe winter
Song Yuanwen
Black and white woodcut
44.5 × 69.5(cm) 1998

天潮　宋源文　黑白木刻
The heavenly tide
Song Yuanwen
Black and white woodcut
46 × 80(cm) 2002

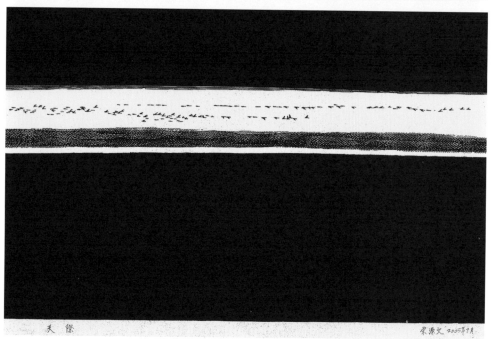

天际　宋源文　黑白木刻
Horizon
Song Yuanwen
Black and white woodcut
46 × 73(cm) 2005

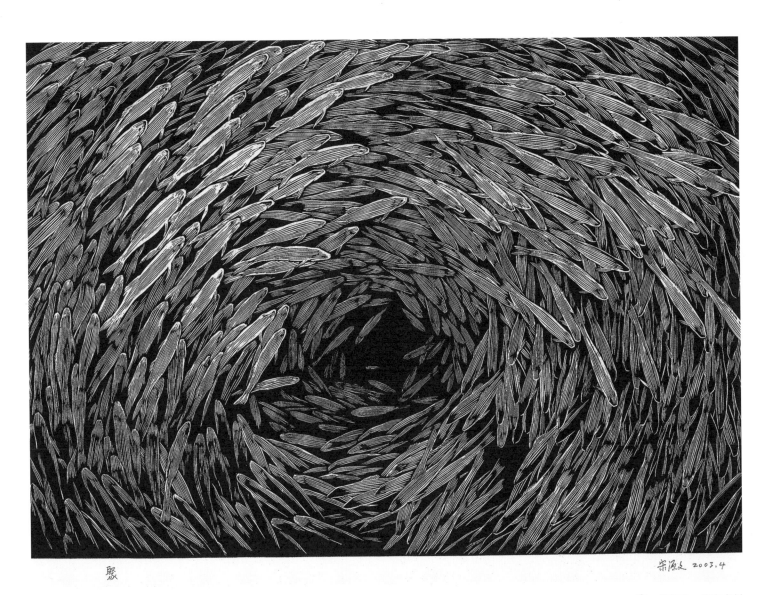

聚

聚　宋源文　黑白木刻
Gathering in
Song Yuanwen
Black and white woodcut
54 × 78(cm)　2003

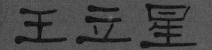
王立星

王立星（1957—　），辽宁抚顺人。1978年就读于抚顺外语师范学校。1980至89年在中学及大学任教，期间毕业于教育学院艺术专业。1989年—1991年在中央美院版画系进修。1991—1994年考入西安美院版画系攻读硕士学位。1994—1995年公派赴英国ULSTER大学进修，1997年至今任职深圳画院。专职画家，中国美术家协会会员，中国版画家协会会员。

Wang Lixing (1957-　), born in Fushun, Liaoning.
Wang graduated from The Fushun Foreign Languages Normal School in 1978, between 1980 and 1989 he held teaching posts in both secondary and higher education, during this time he graduated from the Institute of Education as an arts specialist. Between 1989 and 1991 Wang undertook further study in The Central Academy of Fine Arts Printmaking Department, in 1991 he was accepted to study for an MA degree in Printmaking at The Xian Academy of Fine Arts. During the 1994-1995 academic year he attended The University of Ulster for further study. Since 1997 he has held a post at The Shenzhen Art Academy. A specialist artist, Member of The Chinese Artist's Association, Member of The Chinese Printmaker's Association.

联系电话 Telephone (86) 13556868606
电子信箱 E-mail　　Lixing_wang@sohu.com

1994 年版画《丑角》获第五届全国三版展铜奖

1999 年中国版画家协会颁发"鲁迅版画奖"

2001 年版画《家训》英国北爱尔兰当代中国艺术家邀请
展 MSA 大奖

2003 年公益广告片《永远的罗布泊》获中国第八届国际
广告节大奖

2004 年壁画《清源》广东国庆 55 周年美展优秀奖

PRIZES AWARDED

1994 The 5th National Exhibition of the Three Printmaking
Techniques, Bronze medal for the work 'Clowns'

1999 'Lu Xun Print Award' by Chinese Print Artists' Association

2001 'Family Instructions', MSA Award, by the Inviting
Exhibition of Contemporary Chinese Artists, North Ireland

2003 'Luo Bu Lake Forever', Public Advertisement, won the
Award by the 8th International Advertisement Festival of
China

2004 'Pure Spring', Mural, Excellent Award by the Exhibition
Celebrating the 55th National Day, Guangdong

污染报告之二   王立星   石版
Pollution report II
Wang Lixing
Lithograph
22 × 30(cm) 1992

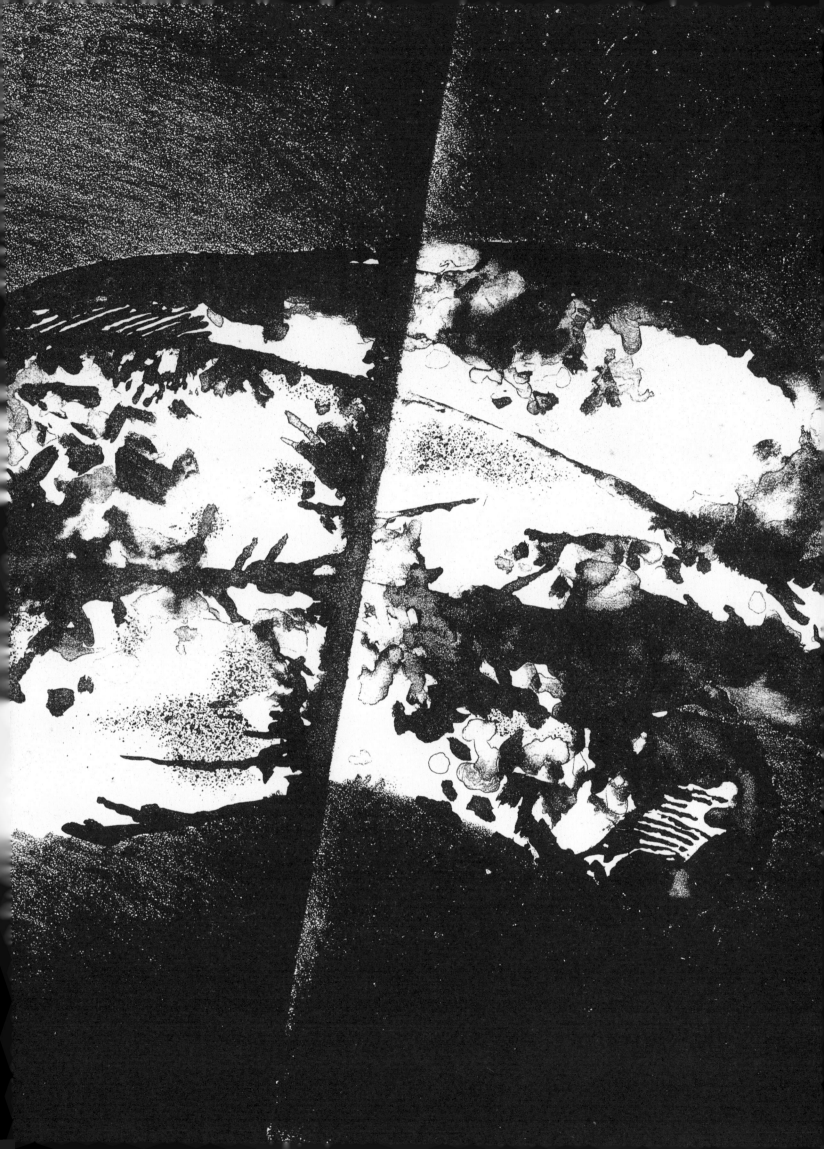

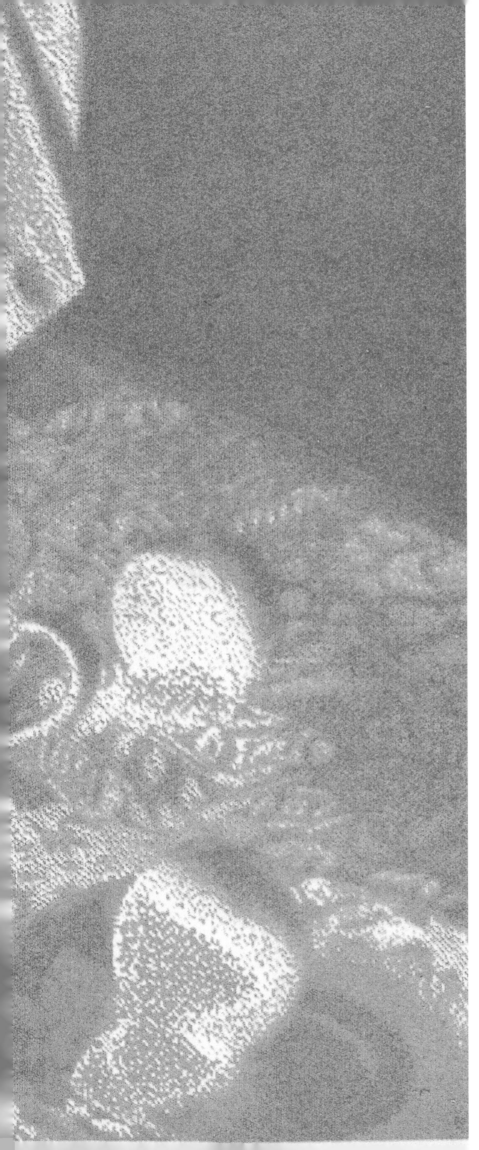

收藏记录

版画《家训》中国美术馆收藏

版画《慧咏》广东美术馆收藏

版画《女孩》英国 ULSTER 艺术中心收藏

彩墨二幅《神仙》德国纽伦堡美术院收藏

版画《蔚蓝色》上海美术馆收藏

版画《静物之二》英国 ULSTER 大学收藏

版画《静物》湖北美院收藏

版画《手掌》西安美院收藏

版画《城市印章》深圳美术馆收藏

水墨《风景》深圳美术馆收藏

版画《家乡》深圳美术馆收藏

版画《冻土》深圳画院收藏

2005 年 15 幅作品被加拿大收藏并编入《中国版画卷》

出版纪录

王立星公共空间艺术作品集，王立星版画、水墨、油彩作品集。

WORKS IN THE COLLECTIONS OF

'Family Instructions', Print, China Museum of Art

'Sound of Wisdom', Print, Guang Dong Museum of Art

'Girl', Print, Fine Art Cenetre of University of Ulster's

'Immotal', 2pc, Colored Ink Painting, Kunst Haus, Germany

'Blue', Oil Painting, Shang Hai Museum of Art

'Still Life ll', Print, University of Ulster's, UK

'Sound of Wisdom', Print, China Academy of Fine Art

'Still Life', Print, Hu Bei Academy of Fine Art

'Palm', Print, Xi'an Academy of Fine Art

'City Seal', Print, Shenzhen Museum of Art

'Landscape', Ink Painting, Shenzhen Museum of Art

'Home', Print, Shenzhen Museum of Art

'Iced Land', Print, Shenzhen Fine of Art

2005 15pc of works are collected in Canada and published in 'Print in China'

静物之三 王立星 丝网
Still life III
Wang Lixing
Screen print
15 × 23.5(cm) 1994

静物三一

画家心语

我崇尚艺术语言上的极端，语言的创造性和不可模仿重复性，正是艺术家独特的个性所在。没有独特的个性强烈的艺术表达方式，是经不起考验的，其艺术生命也一定是短暂的。在我们身边可以造成印痕的版材很多，表达一般性语言还是很充分的，但要做到拓宽思路并在实践中总结，发现更新的语言表达方式来运用到版画创作中，则需要对版画语言特性的深层研究和理解。掌握某种新材料或手段的独立性，以无可取代的表现优势为前提，更需要和艺术家的情感指向，审美理想及精神思考相适应。也就是说，必须通过再创造，进入艺术审美的高层次，才能真正转化为艺术语言而且这种语言也会具备鲜明的独特性。语言特性除物质性表达外，更高的是精神性的赋予，而大师的作品正是那种精神性的力量占第一位的。这种可贵的精神性超越了时代，达到更高的境界。

ARTIST'S STATEMENT

I advocate extreme points in creative language, the creativity of the language and that it cannot be copied or duplicated, this is where the artist's distinctive individuality lies. Without the strength of a distinctive artistically expressive style, the work will not stand the test and artistic life will certainly also be brief. There are so many materials around us for making marks on blocks for printing, to express a basic language is still quite sufficient, yet if ones wishes to develop a broader train of thought and make a summary of practice, one must seek out an even newer language of expressive style to utilise in the creation of prints, one must carry out in depth research and understanding relative to printmaking's unique language. One must master certain kinds of new materials or the medium's independent character, by the expression of control being the working principle that cannot be replaced, it must even be in harmony with the artist's emotional direction, beautiful ideals and spiritual reflections will be formed. One might also say it is necessary to pass through a re-creativity to enter the highest level of artistic beauty, even be able to genuinely transform artistic language moreover this language is also able to possess fresh characteristics. The uniqueness of the language, apart from its expression of materiality, is to a greater degree its being entrusted with spirituality, the work of the masters truly occupy the number one position in the strength of their spirituality. This valuable spirituality transcends time, reaching an even higher realm.

静物之一　王立星　石版＋丝网
Still life I
Wang Lixing
Lithograph and screen print
31.5 × 47(cm) 1995

王立星是一位看似粗放、实则精细，看似随意，实则严谨、且勤勉的艺术家。他在国内外接受过系统的专业教育，思维敏捷，观念现代。近年涉猎广泛，设计、建筑、写作等方面都表现不俗。从其版画作品中能隐约窥探到他收敛了许多平日里的张扬及文静后面的粗野。作品的专业品质过硬，艺术主张特而不群，其眼中的版画更像是实验绘画中的一种间歇，看不出他过分追求复数；更像是在享受平面印刷带来的快感与境界，难怪他说很害怕仅看出自己作品里的主张，而感受不到艺术表达。立星是位有条件长久沉积下来的人，尽管他时常带有一点漫不经心的嫌疑，这也许正是艺术家体验到了某种活性物质以后的精神飞跃，我愿意相信这一点。

ARTISTIC APPRECIATION

Wang Lixing appears to be a crude maker of prints, but is in reality meticulous, he appears to be clumsy yet in reality has a careful understanding, even a diligent printmaker. He has received specialist training both inside and outside China, he has nimble thinking and a sense of the contemporary. In recent years his work has encompassed aspects of design, building and writing all appearing refined. From within his prints one can faintly glean the background roughness softened by everyday life that lies behind Wang's gentle quietness. The specialist quality of the work is able to pass any test, his artistic stance is not a common one, in his eyes printmaking even appears like an intermission in his experimentation with art, without realising the complexity of duplicability, even appearing to enjoy the delight and realm that aspects of printing bring, no wonder he is afraid that his own work shows only the concept he wishes to achieve without showing the artistic impact. Lixing is a person whose terms of reference have been laid down over a long period of time, not hesitating to often carry a little careless suspicion, this also is very likely a spiritual leap arrived at after the artist's experimentation with various kinds of dynamic material, I can express confidence on that point.

静物之二　王立星　石版＋丝网
Still life II
Wang Lixing
Lithograph and screen print
31.5 × 47(cm) 1995

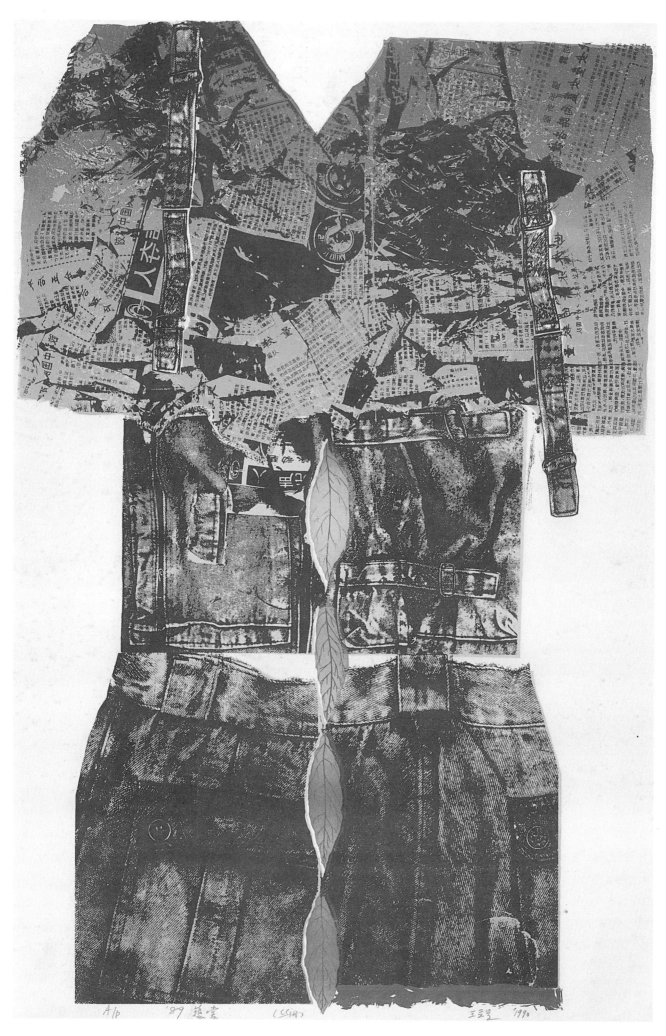

A/p   '89 盐噗   (丝网)   王立星 '1990

8/15　　污染报告之四　　　　　　王立星 1992

污染报告之四　王立星　石版
Pollution report IV
Wang Lixing
Lithograph
22 × 30(cm) 1992

◄ **艺裳**　王立星　丝网版
The crafted skirt
Wang Lixing
Screen print
71 × 46(cm) 1990

◀ **扑克牌** 王立星 丝网
Poker card
Wang Lixing
Screen print
56 × 37(cm) 1994

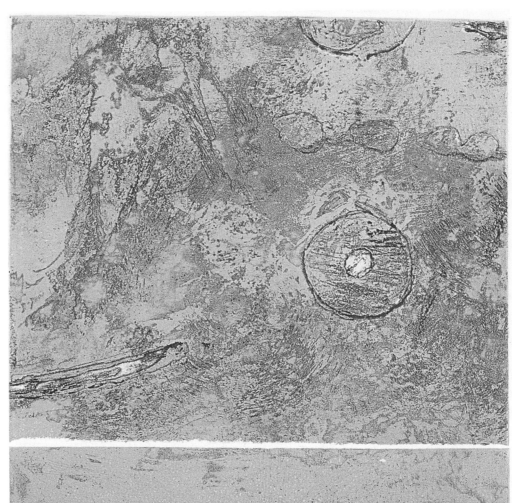

风景 王立星 铜版
Scenery
Wang Lixing
Etching
16 × 28.5(cm) 1999

家训 王立星 铜版
Family precepts
Wang Lixing
Etching
47 × 67(cm) 1999

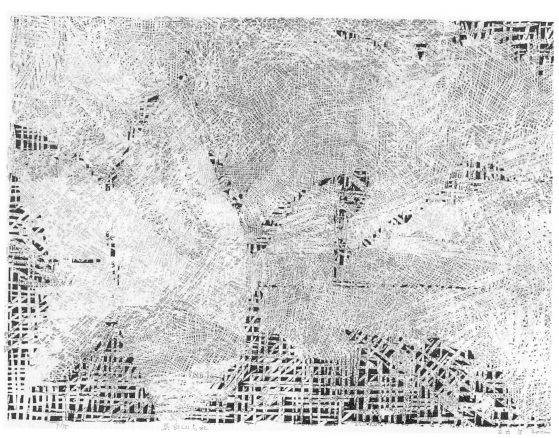

长白山与水 王立星 木版
Changbai mountains and water
Wang Lixing
Woodcut
46 × 65(cm) 2005

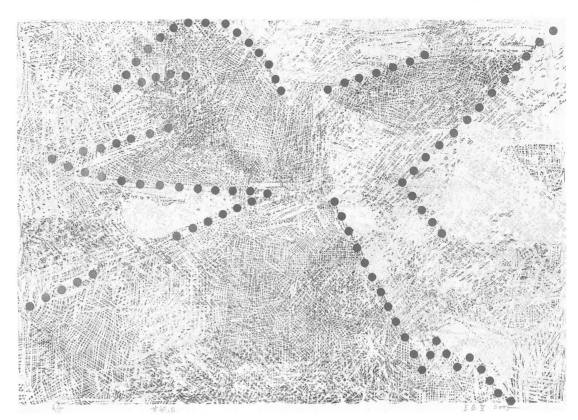

首航日　王立星　木版
The day of the first flight
Wang Lixing
Woodcut
46 × 65(cm) 2005

冻土之二　王立星　木版
Frozen earth II
Wang Lixing
Woodcut
46 × 65(cm) 2005

湿地之三　王立星　木版
Marsh III
Wang Lixing
Woodcut
46 × 65(cm)　2005

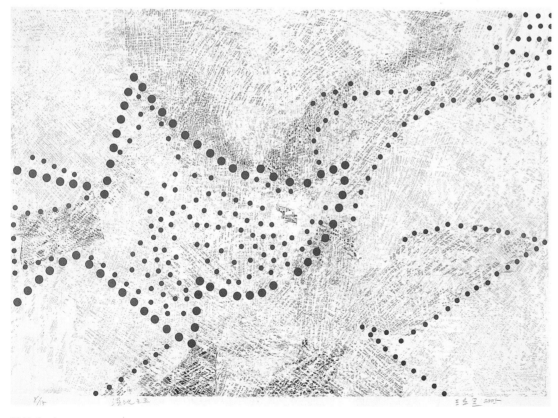

湿地之五　王立星　木版
Marsh IV
Wang Lixing
Woodcut
46 × 65(cm)　2005

▶ 桂林山与水　王立星　木版
Guilin mountain and water
Wang Lixing
Woodcut
65 × 46(cm)　2005

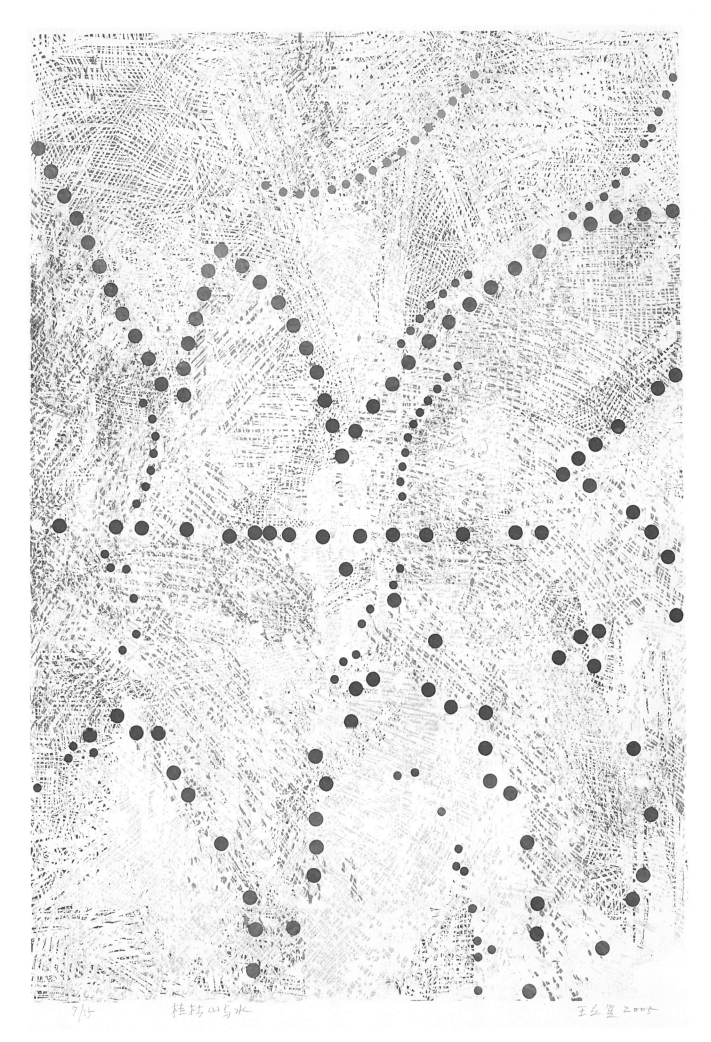

7/17 桂林山与水 王立星 2005

王连敏

王连敏（1962—　　　），吉林长春人。1988 年毕业于吉林艺术学院，现任东北师范大学美术学院教授、中国美术家协会会员、中国版画家协会会员、吉林省美术家协会版画艺术委员会秘书长。

Wang Lianmin (1962-　)，　born in Changchun，Jilin.

Wang graduated from The Jilin Academy of Arts in 1988, he is currently a Professor in The Academy of Fine Art in The North-East Normal University, a member of the Chinese Artist's Association, a member of the Chinese Printmaker's Association and Secretary-General of The Jilin Provincial Artist's Association Printmaking Committee.

联系电话 Telephone (86) 13556868606

1994 年第十二届全国版画展铜奖、1997 年第六届全国三版展优秀
作品奖、1998 年第十四届全国版画展银奖、2000 年第十五届全国
版画展铜奖、2001 年第七届全国三版展银奖、2002 年第十六届全
国版画展金奖、2003 年北京国际版画双年展铜奖、第二届中国美
术金彩奖优秀作品奖、第八届全国三版展银奖。

PRIZES AWARDED

1994 The 12th National Printmaking Exhibition, Bronze medal

1997 The 6th National Exhibition of Three Printmaking Techniques,
    Prize for Outstanding Work

1998 The 14th National Printmaking Exhibition, Silver medal

2000 The 15th National Printmaking Exhibition, Bronze medal

2001 The 7th National Exhibition of Three Printmaking Techniques,
    Silver medal

2002 The 16th National Printmaking Exhibition, Gold medal

2003 The Beijing International Print Biennale, Bronze medal

2003 The 2nd China Fine Art Golden Medal, Prize for Outstanding
    Work

2003 The 8th National Exhibition of Three Printmaking Techniques,
    Silver medal

长白山女　王连敏　铜版
Changbai mountains women
Wang Lianmin
Etching
41 × 46(cm) 1993

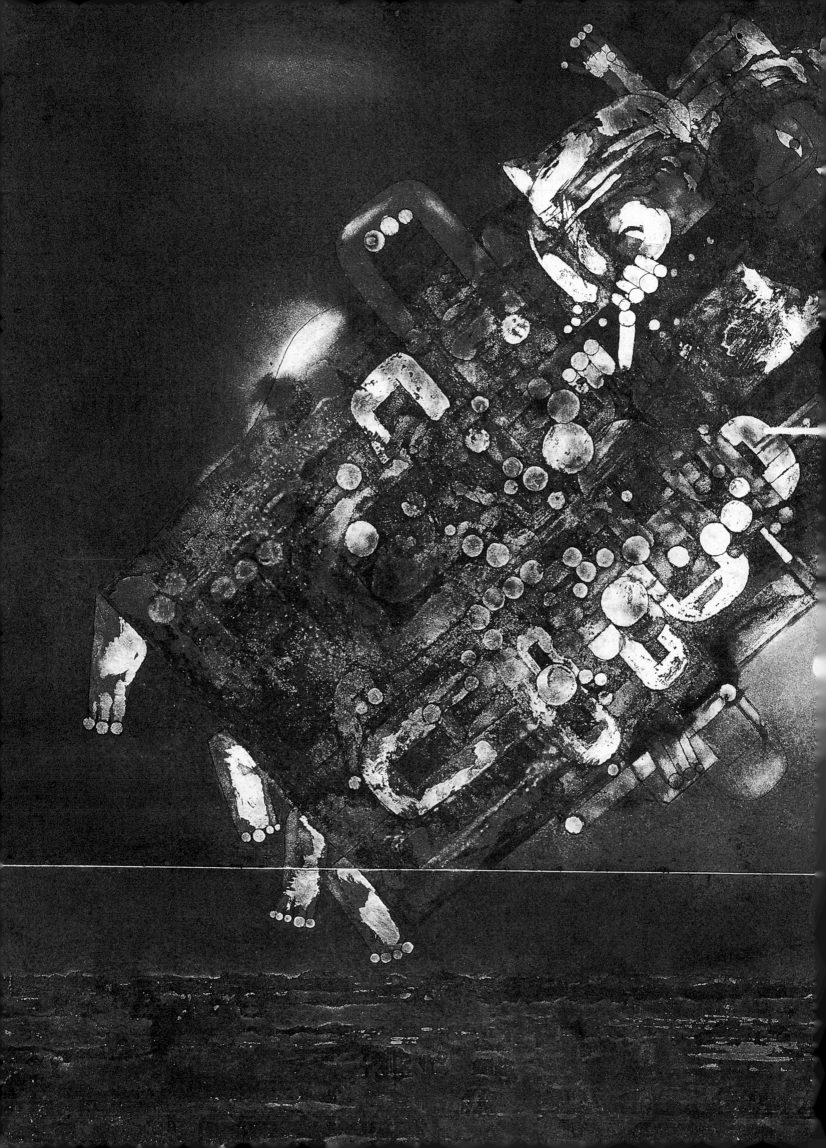

收藏记录

江苏省美术馆、广东美术馆、四川神州版画博物馆、深圳美术馆等。

出版记录

《王连敏铜版画作品集》。

WORKS IN THE COLLECTION OF

The Jiangsu Provincial Gallery of Fine Art

The Guangdong Gallery of Fine Art

The Shenzhou Museum of Printmaking, Sichuan

The Shenzhen Gallery of Fine Art

PUBLICATIONS

A Collection of Etchings by Wang Lianmin

梦之恋　王连敏　铜版
Dream of longing
Wang Lianmin
Etching
49.5 × 56.3(cm) 1996

画家心语

追求作品的精神内涵和表现形式的和谐与完善，是我版画创作的宗旨。语言的深化定会拓展语境的空间。采用不断创新的金属高温固锡工艺，结合传统的铜版技法，加上作者的个性化设计，使画面语言能够充分地表现自我对艺术的深层次思考，作品的精神内涵和理性化的阐述：人类内心情感的深刻体验，生命价值和生存观念的自我感受以及人类与自然和谐与平衡的展示。从中探索艺术风格的独特视角。

ARTIST'S STATEMENT

The aims of my creative work in printmaking is to seek spiritual connotations and to show stylistic harmony and improvements. A deepening of language is really able to broaden the contextual space. In continually using the creative novelty of the craft of high temperature metal working combined with traditional etching techniques supplanted by the artist's individual design, making a pictorial language able to fully demonstrate one's own deep, thoughtful reflections on the arts, the spiritual connotations of the work and the elaboration of one's rationale: the emotions in the hearts of human beings from profound learning through practice, an expression of personal feelings along with a harmony and balance between human beings and nature in respect of the value of life and the sense of existence, from within these elements to explore the unique visual angles of artistic style.

生物恋系列—对话　王连敏　铜版
A love of living things series – Dialogue
Wang Lianmin
Etching
70 × 79(cm)　2002

艺术评介

王连敏是近年崭露头角的青年优秀铜版画家。他在全国版画大展中连连获奖的作品，既提高了铜版画在版画品类中的地位，也扩大了他自己的影响。他的版画创作植根于中华民族传统文化的沃土中，但又倾心于在现代主义表现手法的探索中实现对个性品质的确立，在独特生命体验的表现中实现对人类生存状态及生命价值的考问。其中的音乐人系列人与乐器融合，梦幻与现实对接，其超验奇特的语境虽有些晦涩，但却蕴含着可以解读的丰富性。近年获全国版画展金奖的生物恋系列以超时空的手法，指向宇宙天空海洋，表现人类与自然生物的和谐与矛盾，体现出画家对人类生存环境的关注与焦虑。

ARTISTIC APPRECIATION

Wang Lianmin is a young etcher who has shown a remarkable emerging ability in recent years. In the major national exhibitions of printmaking he has been awarded prizes for his work time after time as well as raising the profile of etching within the field of printmaking, he has also broadened his own influences. His creative work in printmaking has sown roots in the fertile soil of China's traditional culture, yet Wang admires the search to bring about the expression of technique in modernism in respect of the establishment of individual character, to bring about the expression of personal practical learning in respect of the state of human existence and an examination of the value of life. In his series of prints about musicians Wang blends together the figure and the music instruments, dream and reality meet together, its transcendent, singular context although being somewhat obscure, nevertheless contains the possibilities of being understood in its richness. In recent years Wang has been awarded the Gold medal at The National Printmaking Exhibition for the series 'In love with human beings' in which he transcends the technicalities of time and space, pointing towards the great oceans of the cosmos, expressing the harmony and the contradictions between human beings and nature revealing the artist's concerns and anxieties towards the living conditions of humanity.

生物恋系列—信风　王连敏　铜版
A love of living things series – Trade winds
Wang Lianmin
Etching
64.5 × 75(cm)　2003

乐手（二） 王连敏 铜版
Musician II
Wang Lianmin
Etching
48 × 44.5(cm) 1993

乐手 王连敏 铜版
Musician
Wang Lianmin
Etching
45.5 × 45.5(cm) 1994

挽笛 王连敏　铜版
Holding the flute
Wang Lianmin
Etching
42 × 38(cm)　1994

山里的毛毛树 王连敏　铜版
Young tree in the mountains
Wang Lianmin
Etching
41.5 × 42.5(cm)　1996

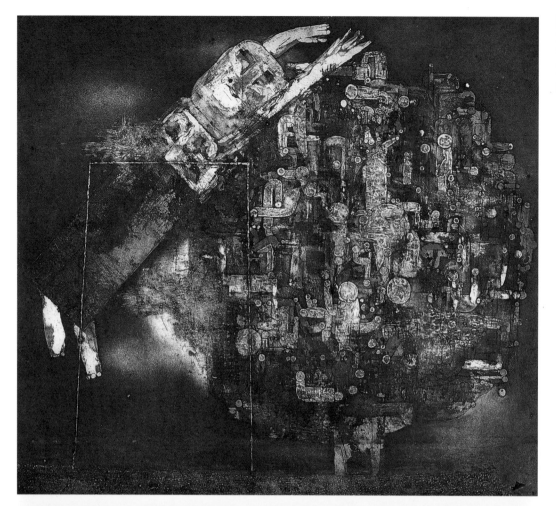

飘　王连敏　铜版
Flutter
Wang Lianmin
Etching
50 × 56(cm)　1997

守护神　王连敏　铜版
Guardian spirit
Wang Lianmin
Etching
50 × 53.5(cm)　1998

偶　王连敏　铜版
Image
Wang Lianmin
Etching
38 × 38(cm)　1999

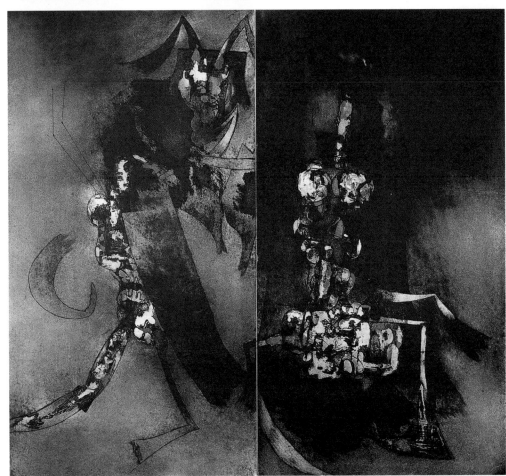

生物恋系列—移化　王连敏　铜版
A love of living things series – Change
Wang Lianmin
Etching
68 × 74.5(cm)　2002

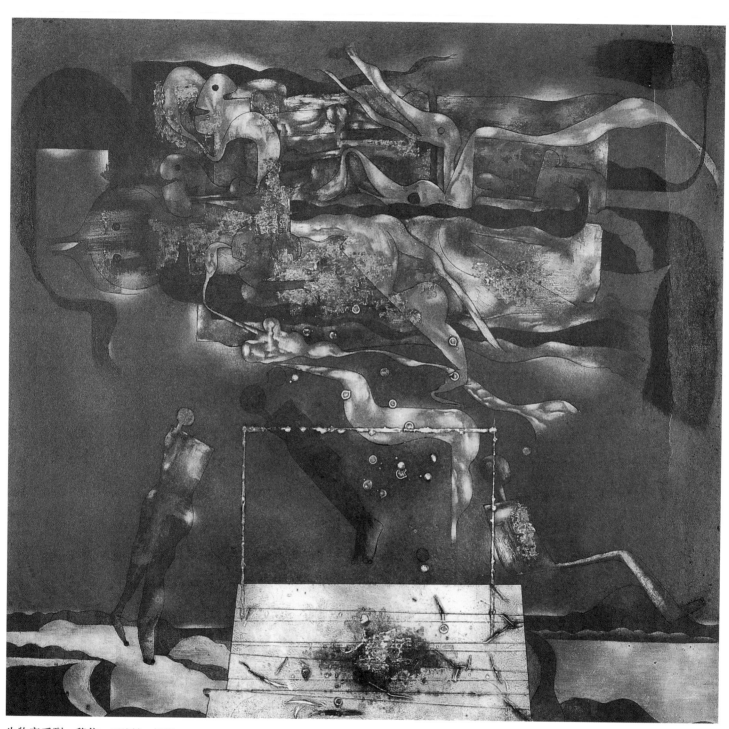

生物恋系列—移位　王连敏　铜版
A love of living things series – Changing places
Wang Lianmin
Etching
75.5 × 79.5(cm) 2003

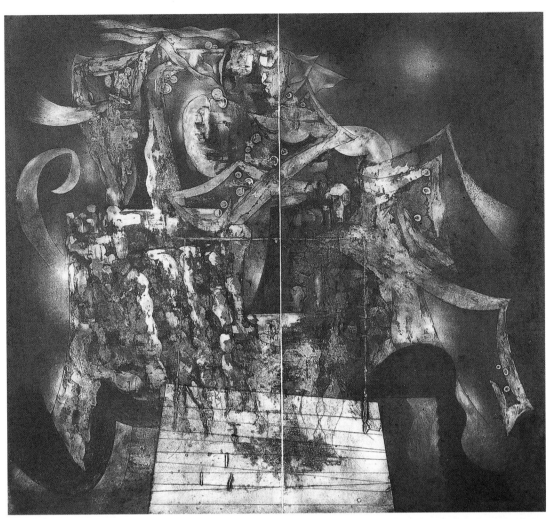

生物恋系列—天鸟　王连敏　铜版
A love of living things series –
Heavenly bird
Wang Lianmin
Etching
65 × 72.5(cm) 2003

颠之歌　王连敏　铜版
Song of the summit
Wang Lianmin
Etching
65.5 × 75.8(cm) 2004

魏谦

魏谦（1946—　　），上海人。曾就读于中央美术学院附中和广州美术学院研究生班。曾任华中师范大学美术系主任、现任华中师大教授、教育部高校艺术类专业教学指导委员会委员、中国美术家协会会员、湖北省美术家协会副主席。

Wei Qian (1946-　　), born in Shanghai.

Wei attended the middle school attached to The Central Academy of Fine Art and graduated from the research group of The Guangzhou Academy of Fine Art. He has held the post of Head of the Department of Fine Art of The Central China Normal University, currently a Professor of The Central China Normal University, a member of The Education Department's Senior Art Specialist Education Guidance Committee, a member of The Chinese Artist's Association and Deputy–Chair of The Hubei Provincial Artist's Association.

联系电话 Telephone (86) 27-67865995

1986 年第九届全国版画展优秀奖、1992 年第十一届全国版画展银奖、1996 年日本·高知第三届国际版画三年展特别奖、1997 年全国第六届铜版、石版、丝网版画展金奖、廖修平奖暨优秀作品奖、1998 年第十四届全国版画展银奖、1999 年第九届全国美展优秀作品奖、1999 年全国"群星奖"美展铜奖、1992 年获国务院颁发的政府特殊津贴，1999 年获"鲁迅版画奖"。

PRIZES AWARDED

1986 The 9th National Printmaking Exhibition, The Prize for Outstanding Work

1992 The 11th National Printmaking Exhibition, Silver Medal

1992 Awarded the State Council promulgated Government Special Subsistence

1996 The 3rd International Print Triennale, Kochi, Japan, Special Prize

1997 The 6th National Exhibition of Etchings, Lithographs and Screen Prints, Gold Medal, The Liao Xiuping Prize and The Prize for Outstanding Work

1998 The 14th National Printmaking Exhibition, Silver Medal

1999 The 9th National Exhibition of Fine Art, The Prize for Outstanding Work

1999 The National Gathering of Stars Prize Exhibition of Fine Art, Bronze Medal

1999 Awarded the Luxun Printmaking Prize'

拣贝壳的女孩　魏谦　铜版
A girl choosing shellfish
Wei Qian
Etching
37.2 × 49(cm) 1987

帕米尔草滩　魏谦　铜版
Pamir grass lands
Wei Qian
Etching
40.5 × 57.5(cm)　1992

"与时俱进"是事物发展的规律，如果中国绘画不能适应社会的发展，不能适应时代的观念变化，不能解决艺术的现代性问题，那将落后于时代，落后于与现代发展相应的人民的精神文化需求，从而艺术也将失去自己的生命活力和前途。在新世纪的美术创作中，我们应作出更多的探索和贡献。

ARTIST'S STATEMENT

'Follow the times' should be the rule for the development of the subject, if Chinese graphic art is unable to adapt to the developments in society, unable to adapt to the contemporary changes in concepts, unable to find solutions to contemporary problems in art, it will lag behind the times, lag behind in respect to contemporary developments appropriate to the spiritual and cultural needs of the people, furthermore art will loose its own vitality and future. In the creativity of the new century, we ought to work with even more exploration and dedication.

胡杨林　魏谦　铜版
Forest of poplars
Wei Qian
Etching
40 × 59(cm) 1993

魏谦是我国铜版画领域杰出的、高产的画家,他在铜版画创作与人才培养方面都成绩斐然。至今已创作铜版画 140 余幅。大体分两种取向,一种是《胡杨林》、《集市小憩》等西部风情系列,体现出画家边疆 15 年深厚的生活底蕴与几经严格训练扎实的造型基础。另一种则以理性追求见著,《永恒》、《根源的洞察》、《人与大地》、《银河系裂变》、《亚西亚之光》、《移动的中国古代文字》几套组画,是一个精神理性与视觉张力交融的艺术结体,它以现在、过去和未来为主题切入时空背景,以超越一般感觉经验的视觉语汇强化作品的超常氛围,以自然、宇宙及宗教理性转述画家对人类、历史与文化的思考。既具有较强的现代意味又表现出对传统文化精神与视觉惯性的眷恋。

ARTISTIC APPRECIATION

Wei Qian is China's most outstanding etcher, a highly productive printmaker, in both the creating of his etchings and in his fostering of talented people his achievements have been remarkable.

Up until now, he has made more than 140 etchings. The greater part of his work divides into two aims, the first, exemplified by the works 'Forest of poplars', 'A short rest at the country fair' and others in the series of views of the western region of China, is to embody the profound details gleaned from the artist's 15 years of life in the border areas and the already rigorous foundations of modelling acquired during his strict training. The other aim is to present a rational and visible expression as in the works 'Eternal permanence', 'Clearly seen sources', ' Man and the vaste earth' , ' Variations on the Milky Way ', ' The light of western Asia', 'The changing characters of ancient China' and several other groups of works, they are an artistic weave of spiritual, cultural and visual senses, they use the present, the past and the future as subject matter to enter into the background of space and time by the extraordinary atmosphere of the strengthened visual vocabulary of the works, Wei surmounts any normal visual experience, by using the rationale of nature, the cosmos and religion the artist reports his reflections in relation to mankind, history and culture. The work also has a strongly contemporary sentiment and expresses the artist's sentimental attachment to the spirit of traditional culture and visual sensitivity.

集市小憩　魏谦　铜版
A short rest at the country fair
Wei Qian
Etching
41.1 × 62.2(cm) 2002

5/95 帕米尔的阳光（铜版） etching 1984.5 魏谦 Weiqian

帕米尔的阳光 魏谦 铜版
Sunlight on the Pamirs
Wei Qian
Etching
33.2 × 35.4(cm) 1984

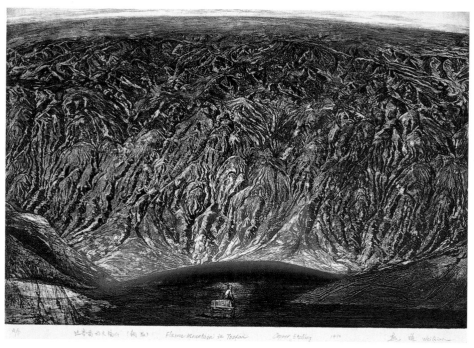

A/P 吐鲁番的火焰山（铜版） Flame Mountain in Tonfan Copper Etching 1992 魏谦 Weiqian

吐鲁番的火焰山 魏谦 铜版
Turfan's fiery mountains
Wei Qian
Etching
37.2 × 56.5(cm) 1992

银河系的裂变 魏谦 铜版
Variations on the Milky Way
Wei Qian
Etching
44 × 50(cm) 1993

观鸟捕蝉图 魏谦 铜版
Watching birds catching cicadas
Wei Qian
Etching
26 × 23.5(cm) 1997

历史的超越—跨越塔克拉玛干 魏谦 铜版
History's transcendence, striding across the Taklamakan
Wei Qian
Etching
60.5 × 85.5(cm) 1998

移动的中国古代文字 魏谦 铜版
The changing characters of ancient China
Wei Qian
Etching
50 × 81(cm) 1998

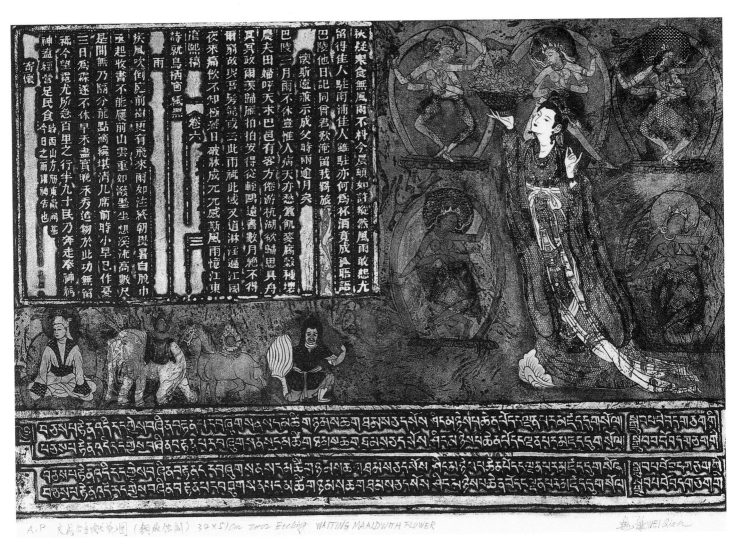

文成公主献花　魏谦　铜版
Fresh flowers for Princess Wen Cheng
Wei Qian
Etching
34 × 51(cm) 2002

快乐的观音菩萨　魏谦　铜版
The smiling Bodhisattva Guan Yin
Wei Qian
Etching
64.5 × 50.6(cm) 2002

圣子 魏谦 铜版
The holy son
Wei Qian
Etching
39 × 51(cm) 2003

天子家族 魏谦 铜版
Imperial clan
Wei Qian
Etching
40.5 × 51(cm) 2004

诗情画意 魏谦 铜版
Poetic charm
Wei Qian
Etching
37.5 × 51(cm) 2004

徐匡

徐匡（1938— ）。湖南长沙人。1958年毕业于中央美术学院附中，现任四川省美术家协会副主席、重庆画家之村艺术委员会主任、中国美术家协会会员、一级美术师。

Xu Kuang (1938-), born in Changsha, Hunan.

Xu graduated from the middle school attached to The Central Academy of Fine Art in 1958, he currently holds the posts of Deputy-Chair of The Sichuan Provincial Artist's Association, Head of The Chongqing Artist's Rural Arts Committee, A Member of The Chinese Artist's Association and A Grade 1 Artist.

8/30　　　陽光下　　　（古川）

阳光下　徐匡　黑白木刻
In the sunlight
Xu Kuang
Black and white woodcut
51 × 67(cm) 1952

WORKS IN THE COLLECTIONS OF

The China Gallery of Fine Art (19 works)

The Norwegian National Museum of Fine Arts

The French National Museum of Fine Arts among other collections.

PUBLICATIONS

'A selection of prints by Xu Kuang'

'A selection of works by Xu Kuang' (Japanese edition)

嘉陵江上　徐匡　黑白木刻
On the Jialing river
Xu Kuang
Black and white woodcut
43 × 59(cm) 1961

画家心语

艺术源于生活，艺术不等于生活。艺术从内容到形式都应该
是健康向上的，给人一种精神上的力量和美的享受。而它又
要与时俱进不断创新，才有生命力。

ARTIST'S STATEMENT

Art is derived from life, but art is not equal to life. From content to
form, art should be spiritually healthy and noble, bringing people
spiritual strength and enjoyment of beauty. At the same time, art
also needs to improve with the progress of the time, constantly
creating new ideas, thus art will achieve vitality.

森林的早晨 徐匡 水印木刻
The early dawns in forest
Xu KuangWoodcut printed with
water-soluble colours
41 × 47(cm) 1979

艺术评介

徐匡素描功底扎实，是位以刻画人物著称、勤奋高产的版画家。20 世纪 50 年代末至 60 年代初属于多方探索阶段，既搞套色油印、水印版画，也搞线刻与大明大暗的黑白版画，还有一批韵味独特的拓片作品，其中《待渡》与《乡村小学》使他初具影响。70 至 80 年代徐匡的版画走向成熟并形成高峰，他把素描调子引入版画，并在《草地诗篇》、《主人》、《高原的阳光》等作品中把这种倾向发展到极致。运用细腻多层次的素描调子，着重外部形态的刻划，使人物具有一种雕塑感、一种强烈的艺术感染力与精神震撼力。此时期徐匡的创作还表现出不同风格追求的跳跃性，有类似工笔白描的《大渡河畔》，有抒情写意的《大河之源》，也有《小骑手》等速写风的版画，这是画家有创造活力的一种表现。但向油画的转向使他中断了版画的探索。

ARTISTIC EVALUATION

Xu Kuang has a very solid drawing ability, he is a prolific artist famed for his depiction of figures. During the late 1950s to the beginning of the 1960s, his work was at a stage of exploration, he made woodcuts with both oil-based ink and water-soluble colour, cut both in line or as chiaroscuro black and white woodcuts. He also created a series of poetic woodcuts using the dabbing technique. Among his works during that period, 'Waiting for the ferry', 'Village school' brought him initial fame. During the 1970s to the 1980s, Xu Kuang's prints matured and formed the peak of his creation, he brought chiaroscuro tones from drawing into woodcut and developed this tendency to an extreme in his 'Poem of the pasture', 'A master' and 'Sunlight of the plateau'. His works use chiaroscuro tones with exquisite multi-layers, stressing the portrayal of form, appearance, giving his figures a sculptural sense, consequently his work has a forceful artistic power and spiritual movement. During this period, Xu's work also showed the intention to explore different styles, 'On the bank of the Dadu River' is in the style of the fine descriptive lines found in traditional 'gongbi' painting, in contrast to the expressive style of 'The fountainhead of the great river'; Xu also employs a sketchy style woodcut like 'The little equestrian', this phenomenon embodies the artist's creative power. However, his change of direction into oil painting ended his exploration of printmaking too early.

洁白的哈达　徐匡　木刻
A spotless Hada scarf
Xu Kuang
Woodcut
65 × 88(cm) 1984

学习 徐匡 黑白木刻
Studying
Xu Kuang
Black and white woodcut
37 × 56(cm) 1960

乡村小学 徐匡 套色木刻
Primary school in the village
Xu Kuang
Multi-block colour woodcut
43 × 57(cm) 1964

破坏敌人的运输线 徐匡 木刻
Breaking the enemy's lines of supply
Xu Kuang
Woodcut
54 × 72(cm) 1965

小河流水 徐匡 水印木刻
The flowing water of a small river
Xu Kuang
Woodcut printed with water-soluble colours
33 × 46(cm) 1977

主人　徐匡　黑白木刻
Master
Xu Kuang
Black and white woodcut
70 × 70(cm) 1978

纳木湖畔　徐匡　套色木刻
Namu lakeside
Xu Kuang
Multi-block colour woodcut
37 × 52(cm) 1978

大江之源　徐匡　套色木刻
The source of the great river
Xu Kuang
Multi-block colour woodcut
70 × 90(cm) 1979

大渡河畔　徐匡　黑白木刻
Dadu river bank
Xu Kuang
Black and white woodcut
42 × 55(cm)　1980

珠峰儿女　徐匡　拓片
Pearl peak's children
Xu Kuang
Rubbing
40 × 40(cm)　1980

新路 徐匡 黑白木刻
The new road
Xu Kuang
Black and white woodcut
54 × 40(cm) 1980.2

希望 徐匡 黑白木刻
Hoping
Xu Kuang
Black and white woodcut
55 × 67(cm) 1981

徐仲偶

徐仲偶 (1952 —),1982年毕业于四川美术学院绘画系版画专业,并留校任教到2001年,曾担任该校版画专业教研室主任,川音成都美术学院教授。现就职于四川大学艺术学院,为中国美术家协会四川分会理事,中国版画家协会会员,中国工艺美术家协会会员,四川美协版画艺委会副主任,四川省美术专业高级技术资格评审委员会委员,成都市美协版画艺委会主任,成都版画艺术院院长。

Xu Zhongou (1952-), born in Chengdu, Sichuan.

Xu graduated from the Painting Department of The Sichuan Academy of Fine Art in 1985 having specialised in Printmaking, remaining at the Academy as a teacher until 2001. Xu was then appointed as Head of the Academy's Printmaking Workshop, a Professor at The Chengdu Chuanyin Academy of Fine Arts. Xu is also presently undertaking duties at The Sichuan University Arts Institute, he is Director of The Sichuan branch of The Chinese Artist's Association, a member of The Chinese Printmaker's Association, a member of The Chinese Arts and Crafts Association, Deputy-Chair of The Sichuan Artist's Association Printmaking Arts Committee, a member of The Sichuan Provincial Fine Arts Specialist Senior Technical Qualification Appraisal Committee, Chair of The Chengdu City Artist's Association Printmaking Arts Committee and Principal of The Chengdu Academy of Printmaking Arts.

联系电话 Telephone (86) 13308034021
电子信箱 E-mail sccdxzo@163.com

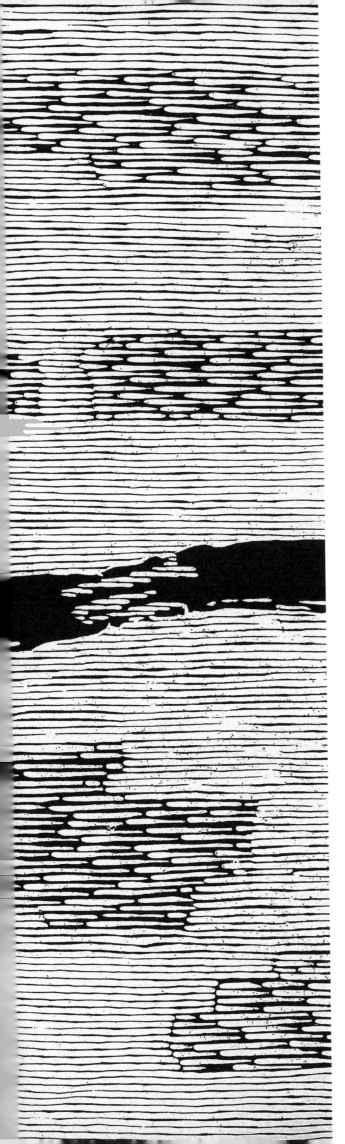

获奖记录

1992 年版画《榫卯系列》获全国第十一届版画作品展铜奖、1996 年版画《长征是一种信念》获纪念中国工农红军长征 60 周年美术作品展一等奖、版画《何时缚住苍龙》获纪念中国工农红军长征 60 周年美术作品展优秀奖、1997 年版画《chant》获 1997 波兰国际版画双年展奖、版画《Hidden》获 1997 年波兰国际版画双年展奖、2004 年版画《土地》获第十届全国美术作品展银奖。

收藏记录

多幅作品被中国美术馆、大英博物馆、美国德克萨斯州布什图书馆、英国欧洲木版画基金会等收藏。

PRIZES AWARDED

1992 The 11th National Printmaking Exhibition, Bronze medal for the 'Mortice and Tenon' series

1996 The Exhibition of Fine Art Commemorating the 60th year of the Chinese Workers and Peasants Red Army Long March, First prize for the work 'The Long March is a kind of faith'

1996 The Exhibition of Fine Art Commemorating the 60th year of the Chinese Workers and Peasants Red Army Long March, Prize for Outstanding Work for the work 'What time do we tie up the giant dragon'

1997 The Polish International Print Biennale Prize for the work 'Chant'

1997 The Polish International Print Biennale Prize for the work 'Hidden'

2004 The 10th National Exhibition of Fine Art, Silver medal for the work 'Earth'

WORKS IN THE COLLECTIONS OF

Many of the artist's works are in the collections of :

The China Gallery of Fine Art

The British Museum

The Bush Library, Texas, USA

The Muban Foundation, London

书写之间—展　徐仲偶　黑白木刻
Writing spaces – unfold
Xu Zhongou
Black and white woodcut
65 × 65(cm) 2004

中国的意象美学影响到我的艺术，中国悠久的历史文化常常让我感叹先民的智慧，同时历史的沉重和人性的困境也常常让我反思生命存在的价值和意义。我的艺术既生长在此时此刻，也生长在历史的漫长中……艺术创作将我生命历程中的快乐和痛苦都融化在了我的作品里。从过去异化、挣扎、彷徨的艺术表达到现在释放、自由与安详地创作，我的生命被基督的光照耀，——此时此刻被点燃，生命变成了在基督的爱里尽心、尽性、尽意的表达。

ARTIST'S STATEMENT

The aesthetics of Chinese imagery have influenced my creative work, China's long historical culture has always encouraged me to proclaim the wisdom of the ancients, at the same time the weight of history and the predicaments of humanity have also frequently allowed me to re-think the value and meaning of life. My creative work has grown out of both this present time and this present moment, it has also grown up within the slow passage of history...... the creation of art in the course of my life, the happiness and the anguish have both blended together in my work. From the expression of an art of an alienation with the past, the struggle, from lacking any sense of direction to the release of today, with independence and serene creativity, my life is illuminated by Jesus' light,--------kindled at this time and at this moment, my life has changed in the love of Jesus, expressed with all my heart, with all my spirit and with all my thoughts.

书写之间　徐仲偶　黑白木刻
Writing spaces
Xu Zhongou
Black and white woodcut
65 × 65(cm)　2004

艺术评介

徐仲偶喜爱中国的传统文化和意象思维，又对西方重视个人体悟，个人视觉经验，个人语言结构的独特性，及由此而生的对传统的反叛性，以及那种特有的视觉形式的冲击力和震撼力感兴趣。兼东西之长而有之成为徐仲偶艺术语言探索的基本思路。他的版画当是一种既不同于西方现当代艺术，又不同于东方的古典传统艺术的一种全新的中国的现代艺术。

ARTISTIC APPRECIATION

Xu Zhongou loves China's traditional culture and visual thinking, he also values the individual realisation in the West, the individual's experience of the visual sense, the distinctiveness of individual structural language, thus giving rise to traditional rebelliousness, moreover a kind of particular form of visual sense, interested in a forceful and dynamic strength. An exploration of the merits of both East and West have become Xu Zhongou's creative language and the basis of his thinking. His prints are both dissimilar to contemporary Western art and dissimilar to Eastern antique traditional art, a kind of completely new Chinese contemporary art.

书写之间—器　徐仲偶　黑白木刻
Writing spaces – implement
Xu Zhongou
Black and white woodcut
65 × 65(cm) 2004

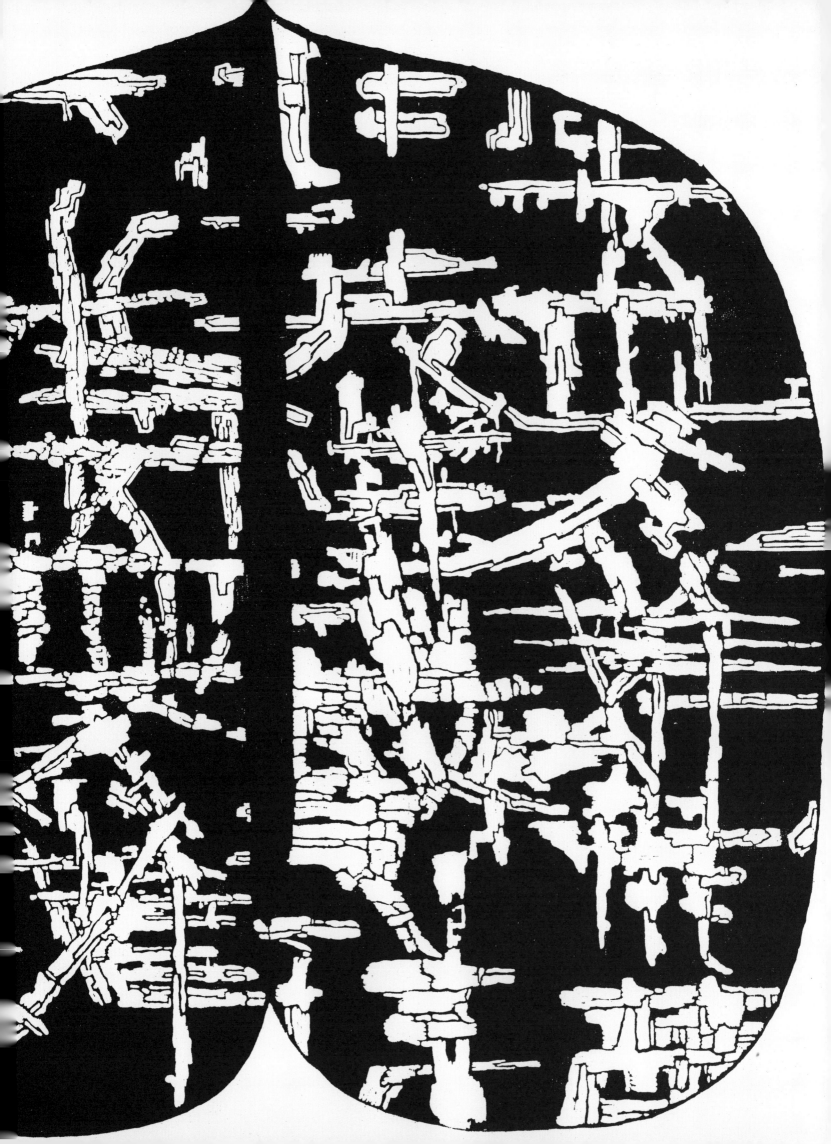

写　徐仲偶　黑白木刻
Description
Xu Zhongou
Black and white woodcut
65 × 65(cm) 2000

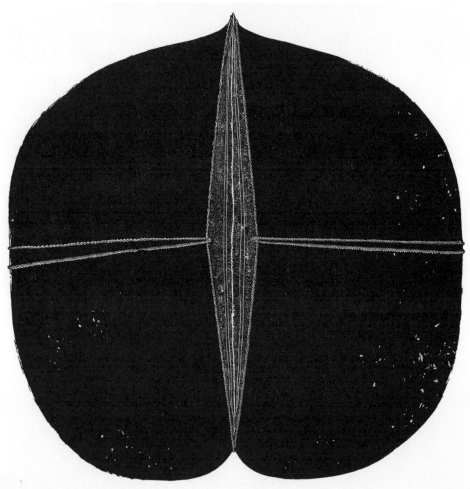

伸　徐仲偶　黑白木刻
Stretch
Xu Zhongou
Black and white woodcut
65 × 65(cm) 2000

影　徐仲偶　黑白木刻
Shadow
Xu Zhongou
Black and white woodcut
60 × 60(cm)　2002

驿　徐仲偶　黑白木刻
Rest house
Xu Zhongou
Black and white woodcut
65 × 65(cm)　2002

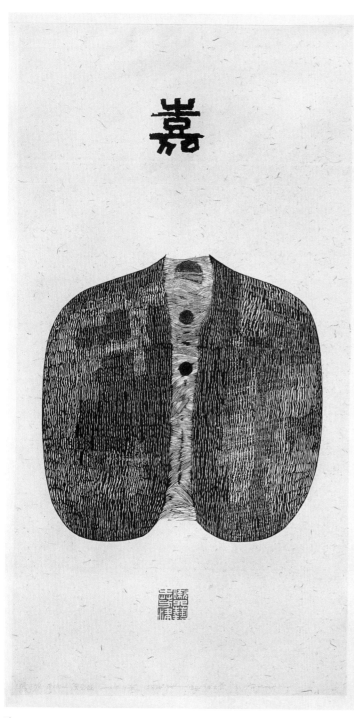

连　徐仲偶　黑白木刻
Connect
Xu Zhongou
Black and white woodcut
136 × 68(cm)　2002

写　徐仲偶　黑白木刻
Description
Xu Zhongou
Black and white woodcut
130 × 65(cm)　2002

仰　徐仲偶　黑白木刻
Admiration
Xu Zhongou
Black and white woodcut
140 × 67(cm) 2003

桥　徐仲偶　黑白木刻
Bridge
Xu Zhongou
Black and white woodcut
140 × 70(cm) 2003

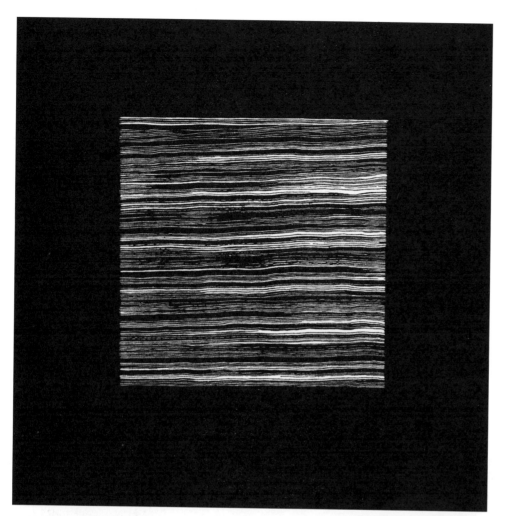

流　徐仲偶　黑白木刻
Flow
Xu Zhongou
Black and white woodcut
61 × 61(cm) 2004

峡　徐仲偶　黑白木刻
Pass
Xu Zhongou
Black and white woodcut
65 × 65(cm) 2004

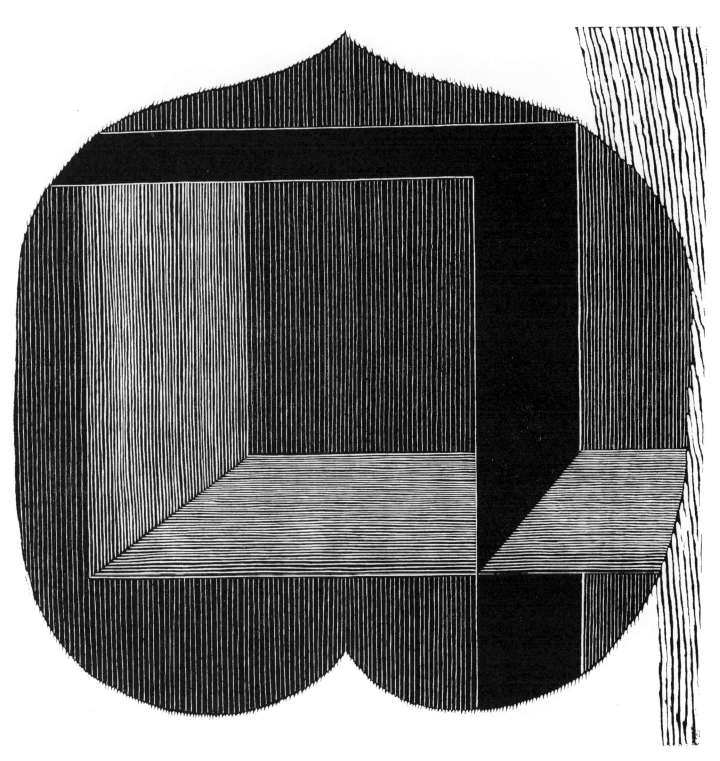

间　徐仲偶　黑白木刻
Space
Xu Zhongou
Black and white woodcut
65 × 65(cm)　2004

叠　徐仲偶　黑白木刻
Pile up
Xu Zhongou
Black and white woodcut
65 × 65(cm)　2004

窜　徐仲偶　黑白木刻
Exile
Xu Zhongou
Black and white woodcut
71 × 69(cm) 2004

郑爽

郑爽（1937— ），福建人。1962 年毕业于中央美术学院版画系。曾任中国美术家协会常务理事、广东省美协副主席。现为广州美术学院教授，中国美术家协会版画艺术委员会委员，广东美术家协会常务理事、版画艺委会主任。

Zheng Shuang (1937-), born in Fujian.

In 1962 Zheng graduated from The Printmaking Department of The Central Academy of Fine Arts.She was assigned to The Chinese Artist's Association as Managing Director, then as Deputy Chair of The Guangdong Provincial Artist's Association. She is currently a Professor (retired) in The Guangzhou Academy of Fine Arts, a committee member of The Chinese Artist's Association Printmaking Committee, Manager of The Guangdong Artist's Association, Chair of The Printmaking Committee.

联系电话 Telephone (86) 20-84017778

获奖记录

1982 年法国春季沙龙展金奖、1984 年第六届全国美展两项
银奖、1987 年世界文化荟萃（阿尔及利亚）集体特别金奖、
1993 年中国版画版种大展铜奖。

PRIZES AWARDED

1982 A gold medal from the French Spring Salon Exhibition

1984 Two silver medals from The 6th National Exhibition of Fine Art

1987 Special gold medal from The World Cultural Gathering (Algeria)
     Collective

1993 Bronze medal, Chinese Printmaking Major Exhibition

勿忘我　郑爽　水印木刻
Forget - me - not
Zheng Shuang
Woodcut printed with water-soluble colours
32.8 × 20(cm)　1982

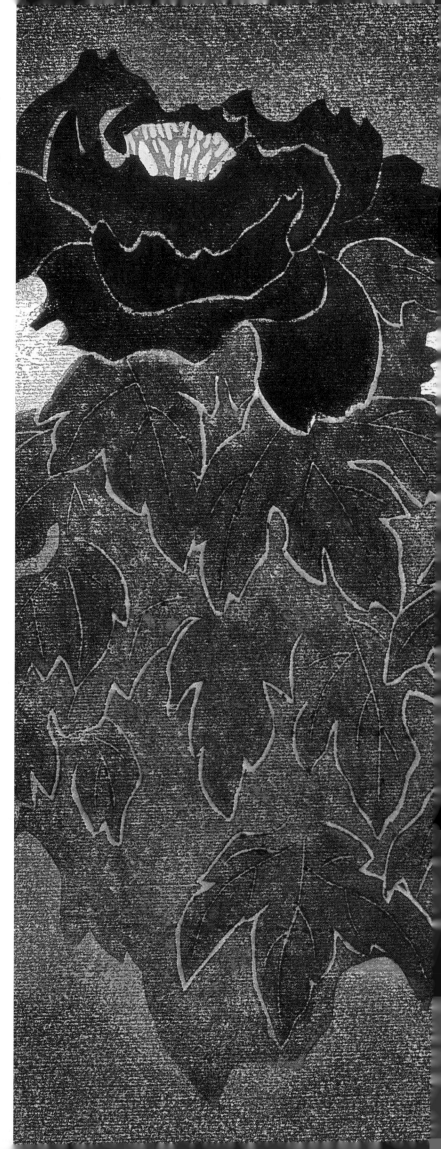

黑牡丹白牡丹　郑爽　水印木刻
Black peony, white peony
, Zheng Shuang
Woodcut printed with water soluble colours
52 × 72.5(cm) 1984

永远的星星

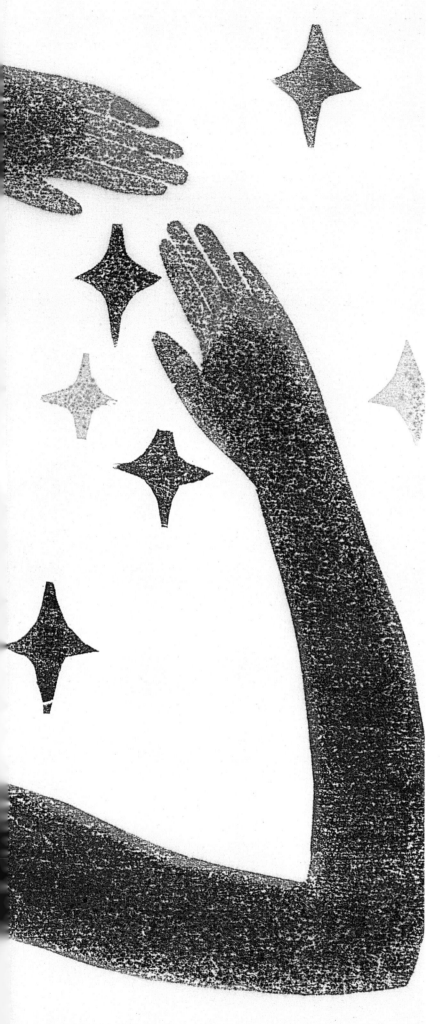

我希望我的画能给人带来愉快，给人带来安慰。它们不是什么大作，也没什么特别的"思想性"和"教育意义"，但它能给人们以愉快和美的享受，使人感到亲切温暖。如果你心情不好，看到它们能使你愉快，如果你的房间暗淡，挂上它能使之增加一点生气，能做到这一点，我就很高兴了。我自知做不了大树，我只是路边的小草、野花，它们给大地带来生命，覆盖黄土，装点道路，我想这是我的使命。

ARTIST'S STATEMENT

I hope my work is able to bring pleasure to people, give people comfort. They are not great works, there are no special 'thoughts' or 'educational meanings', but they can bring people happiness and an enjoyment of beauty, making people feel friendly and warm. If you are in bad humour, looking at my work may lift your mood, if your room is gloomy, hanging one of my works may bring a little dynamism, if my work can do this, I will be very pleased. I know myself that I cannot become a giant tree, I am just a blade of grass beside the road, a wild flower, yet even they can bring life to the land, cover the yellow earth, decorate the road, I think this is my mission.

永远的星星　郑爽　水印木刻
Eternal star
Zheng Shuang
Woodcut printed with water-soluble colours
36.8 × 48.8(cm) 1986

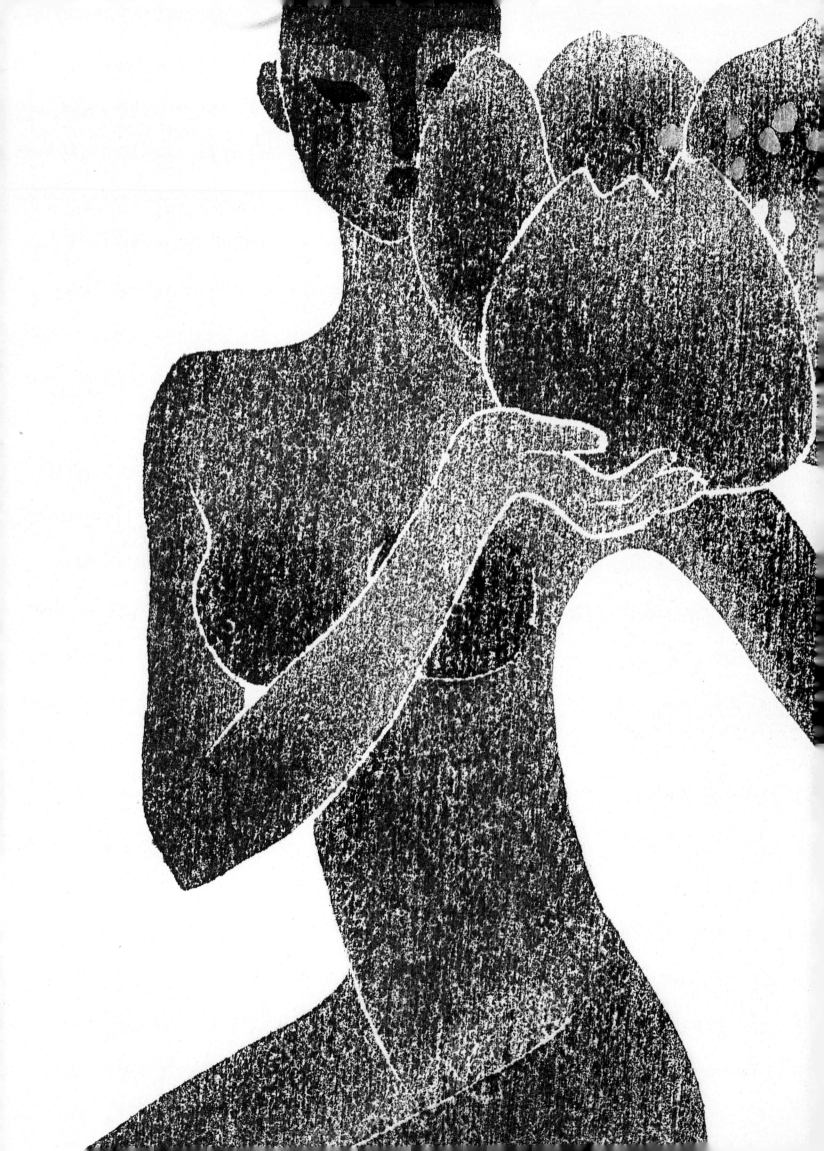

郑爽是广东版画创作的骨干与主要的组织领导者。她长于水印木刻，喜欢刻划静物，尤善花卉，作品注重情趣的表现，韵味独特，格调秀媚。其代表作《绣球花》入选法国春季沙龙展并获金奖，《黑牡丹、白牡丹》在第六届全国美术作品展览中获银奖，使题材平凡、样式小巧的花卉版画地位提升，令人刮目相看。郑爽对花有特殊的感情，她以女性特有的感受与柔情处理花卉与猫咪等题材，一幅幅版画像一首首小诗与童话，浪漫而抒情。她的人物版画《龙的传人》以及《永远的流星》、《我是那清清的流水》等，也造型简括，设色淡雅，充满幻想的情趣。欣赏她的作品会使性情受到陶冶，心灵得到净化，在平和怡然之中得到美的享受。

ARTISTIC EVALUATION

Zheng Shuang is the mainstay, leader and organizer of printmaking in Guangdong province. Her expertise is with woodcut printmaking with water-soluble colours, she particularly likes to depict still life, especially flowers, the work's most important concerns are expression, lingering charm, uniqueness, a prettiness of style. Her representative work 'Big leaf hydrangea' was shown at the French Spring Salon and won a gold medal; the print 'Black peony and white peony' won a silver medal at the 6th China National Art Exhibition, raising the status of small, delicate prints with flowers as their subject matter, encouraging people to look at this kind of work with new eyes. Zheng Shuang has special affection for flowers, she deals with the subject matter of flowers and cats with a unique feminine feeling and tenderness, every print is like a short poem or fairy tale, romantic and lyrical. Her prints with figures such as 'The offspring of a dragon', 'Eternal star' and 'I am that sluggish trickle of water' and other works, are also lightly modelled, with a graceful applied colour, full of imaginative appeal. Viewing her work cleanses one's personality, purifies the heart, one enjoys the beauty of her work in a tranquil and carefree mood.

夏日　郑爽　水印木刻
Summer's day
Zheng Shuang
Woodcut printed with water-solubleColours
47.7 × 43(cm)　1988

扶桑扶桑 郑爽 水印木刻
Hibiscus, hibiscus
Zheng Shuang
Woodcut printed with water-soluble colours
59 × 56.5(cm) 1992

古陶 • 壺　郑爽　水印木刻
Ancient ceramic, pot
Zheng Shuang
Woodcut printed with water-soluble colours
46.3 × 45.5(cm) 1994

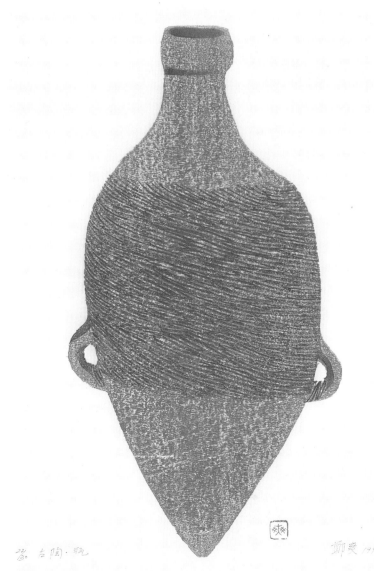

古陶 • 瓶　郑爽　水印木刻
Ancient ceramic, vase
Zheng Shuang
Woodcut printed with water-soluble colours
48.2 × 37(cm) 1994

我有一只小猫叫嘎嘎　郑爽　水印木刻
I have a little cat called Ga Ga
Zheng Shuang
Woodcut printed with water-soluble colours
49.5 × 52.5(cm) 1994

初夏　郑爽　水印木刻
Early summer
Zheng Shuang
Woodcut printed with water-soluble colours
43.5 × 57(cm) 1995

落叶季节　郑爽　水印木刻
The season of falling leaves
Zheng Shuang
Woodcut printed with water-soluble colours
52 × 58(cm) 1995

狮子猫　郑爽　水印木刻
Lion cat
Zheng Shuang
Woodcut printed with water-soluble colours
27.3 × 29.3(cm)　1996

山茶　郑爽　水印木刻
Camellia
Zheng Shuang
Woodcut printed with water-soluble colours
34.7 × 34(cm)　1998

苏格兰的花　郑爽　水印木刻
Scottish flower, thistle
Zheng Shuang
Woodcut printed with water-soluble colours
59.5 × 56(cm)　2000

睡莲花　郑爽　水印木刻
Water - lily
Zheng Shuang
Woodcut printed with water-soluble
colours
25.6 × 29.5(cm)　2000

郁金香　郑爽　水印木刻
Tulip
Zheng Shuang
Woodcut printed with water-soluble
colours
40 × 37(cm)　2002

钟曦

钟曦（1963—　），江西宜春人。1986年毕业于江西师范大学美术系，1989年结业于中央美术学院版画系。现任深圳大学艺术学院教授，艺术教育系主任，中国美术家协会会员，深圳市美术家协会副主席、《中国版画》杂志副主编。

Zhong Xi (1963-　), born in Yichun, Jiangxi.

Zhong graduated from The Department of Fine Art, Jiangxi Normal University in 1986, completing a further course of study at The Central Academy of Fine Art in 1989. He currently holds the posts of Professor at The Academy of Arts, Shenzhen University, Chair of the Faculty of Art Education, Member of the Chinese Artist's Association, Deputy-Chair of The Shenzhen City Artist's Association and Deputy-Editor in Chief of the journal 'China Printmaking'.

联系电话 Telephone　(86) 13902973616

755-83162206

电子信箱 E-mail　　zhongxi@szu.edu.cn

获奖记录

1994 年第十二届全国版画展铜奖、2000 年第十五届全国版画展金奖、2000 年首届青岛·国际版画双年展铜奖、2001 年第七届全国三版展优秀奖、1999 年获鲁迅版画奖。

PRIZES AWARDED

1994 The 12th National Printmaking Exhibition, Bronze medal

1999 Awarded the 'Lu Xun Printmaking Prize'

2000 The 15th National Printmaking Exhibition, Silver medal

2000 The 1st Qingdao International Print Biennale, Bronze medal

2001 The 7th National Exhibition of Three Printmaking Techniques, Prize for Outstanding Work

涓　钟曦　丝网版画
Tiny stream
Zhong Xi
Screen print
80 × 54(cm)　1999

收藏记录

中国美术馆、广东美术馆、青岛美术馆、深圳美术馆等。

出版记录

《钟曦版画作品集》、《画家画语》、《图式与背景》、《名家素描艺术》、《艺术审美简论》。

WORKS IN THE COLLECTIONS OF

The China Gallery of Fine Art

The Guangdong Gallery of Fine Art

The Qingdao Gallery of Fine Art

The Shenzhen Gallery of Fine Art

PUBLICATIONS

'A collection of prints by Zhong Xi'

'The artist speaks about art'

'Graphic form and background'

'Drawings by famous artists'

'Selected talks on the beauty of art'

板块　钟曦　丝网版画
Printing block
Zhong Xi
Screen print
55 × 78(cm)　1999

板块NO.1

78×55 cm　　　　　鐘曦 ZHONGXI　1999年于深圳大学

在现代绘画领域中，视觉符号的构成方式是艺术家沟通人类精神领域的一种具有语言功用的交流形式，也是扩大人类审判范畴，拓展创造性思维的重要手段。

ARTIST'S STATEMENT

In the field of contemporary art practice, the manner of forming the visual image is the artist's link with the realm of the human spirit, having a style of exchange in language function, also expanding the category of human aesthetics, also developing the important medium of creative ideas.

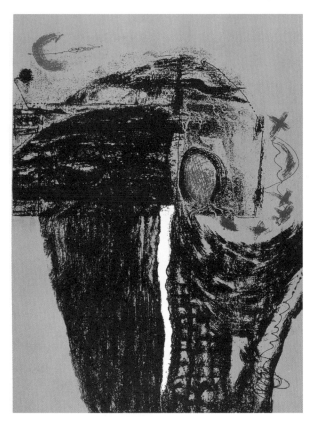

衍生　钟曦　丝网版画
Derive
Zhong Xi
Screen print
60 × 45(cm) 1999

钟曦是我国丝网版画家中的佼佼者，近年他的丝网版画屡屡获奖，尤其是《落差系列——远古与未来》获全国版画展金奖，不仅扩大了他自己的影响，也提高了这一小版种的地位。他的版画创作追求现代品质与观念理性，注重画面视觉符号的研究，1995 年以前创作的《钟声》、《失落的羽毛》等，以对传统文化符号的现代提纯，或通过对自然生态的焦虑与关注，体现画家的人文、现实关怀。此后的《速力系列》、《维度系列》、《生命系列》等，则在理念追逐中实现对泛文化语境的超越，在对速力与空间的把控与放纵之间，实现视觉图式的变革。近期的《悬浮》、《漂》、《透光》、《家谱·元》等则有意摆脱中外丝网版画共存的机印效果与制作感，在随意的绘画性（手绘感）中寻觅个性落点，颇富创造灵性。

ARTISTIC APPRECIATION

Zhong Xi is the leading exponent among China's printmakers employing screen - printing, in recent years his screen prints have repeatedly been awarded prizes among which is the 'Drop in elevation series – remote antiquity and the future ' awarded the Gold Medal at The National Printmaking Exhibition. This award has not only increased his own influence but has also raised the status of this minor form of printmaking. His creative work in printmaking pursues contemporary qualities and a sense of the rational laying stress on research into the visual image; the works created before 1995 'Sound of the bell', 'The lost feather' and other works through a contemporary refinement of traditional cultural symbols or through the means of the anxieties and concerns of one's mode of life reflects the artist's humanity and the reality of caring. The works following this period 'Speed series', 'Dimension series', 'Life series' and others are in the pursuit of ideas to overcome a frigid cultural context, in the control and self-indulgence with speed and space, a transformation of image style. The works of recent times 'Suspension' , 'Floating', 'Penetrating light', 'Family tree-distance' and others are intended to break away from the coexistence of Chinese and foreign screen-prints with their machine printed effects and manufactured looks, to make art of one's own pleasing (a feeling for the hand-crafted), one looks for an individual aiming point, a rich productive intelligence.

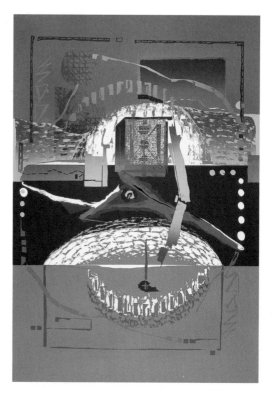

将军令　钟曦　丝网版画
Check !
Zhong Xi
Screen print
67 × 91(cm)　2001

生命系列一　钟曦　丝网版画
Life series I
Zhong Xi
Screen print
80.5 × 41.5(cm)　1999

8/10　生命系列之一　　丝网版画　　钟曦 1999

错位　钟曦　丝网版画
Dislocation
Zhong Xi
Screen print
58 × 42(cm)　1999

夏季的风　钟曦　丝网版画
Summer wind
Zhong Xi
Screen print
68.5 × 45.5(cm)　2000

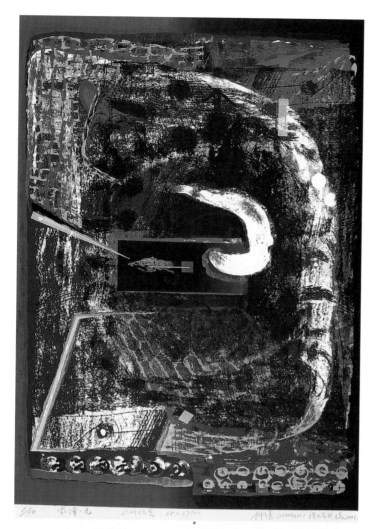

家谱·元　钟曦　丝网版画
Family tree-distance
Zhong Xi
Screen print
65 × 47(cm)　2001

母语　钟曦　丝网版画
Mother's words
Zhong Xi
Screen print
68 × 45(cm)　2001

记忆景观 钟曦 丝网版画
Remembered landscape
Zhong Xi
Screen print
61 × 45.5(cm) 2003

下一站 钟曦 丝网版画
The next stop
Zhong Xi
Screen print
61 × 45.5(cm) 2003

灰色的天空 钟曦 丝网版画
Grey sky
Zhong Xi
Screen print
61 × 45.5(cm) 2003

年代 钟曦 丝网版画
Decade
Zhong Xi
Screen print
61 × 45.5(cm) 2003

近距离　钟曦　丝网版画
Near distance
Zhong Xi
Screen print
61 × 45.5(cm)　2003

黑箱子　钟曦　丝网版画
Black box
Zhong Xi
Screen print
73 × 59(cm)　2003

后记 POSTSCRIPT

作为加拿大北美永新能源有限公司的行政经理,一年多来我配合公司总裁王柏年先生开展此次艺术收藏活动。从此次活动最初的策划,到目前画册的最终出版,一年多的辛苦终于看到了成果,捧着手中的画册,欣喜之情跃然心上。

此次艺术收藏活动在公司总裁王柏年先生的倡议下,得到深圳大学艺术学院齐凤阁院长以及画册中所收藏的16位著名版画家的协助与支持,在与他们的接触过程中,我深切的感受到中国版画家乐于将中国版画艺术介绍给世界的强烈愿望和热情。在此,我也深深地希望此次活动可以帮助他们达成这个美好的愿望!

一年多来,在齐凤阁、其加达瓦、钟曦3位老师的组织下,画册的编委会成员5次相聚在深圳大学,共同探讨画册的排版、印刷,力争拿出最好的作品奉献给中国版画界和全世界热爱版画艺术的朋友!

同时中国版画界的老朋友退休的教授 David Barker 先生承担了此次画册的翻译工作,并于2005年12月亲自来到深圳大学,参与了当时正召开的编委会,为画册的完善提供了宝贵的意见。在此,我深深地向这位热爱中国版画艺术的国际友人致以诚挚的谢意!

在画册的制作过程中,资深摄影师金铁路先生义务承担了此画册的摄影工作,为每幅版画拍摄专业的翻转片,使画册增色不少,在此对金先生提供的帮助表示深深的谢意!

王先生为此次活动专门聘请了上海大学美术学院刘双先生奔波各地,为画家、画册赞助方拍照,在此深表谢意!

在画册的出版印刷过程中,我们得到了国内印刷界的知名企业——雅昌企业(集团)有限公司的大力支持。董事长万捷先生在了解了"爱我中华"的主题后,调动了公司多名优秀的人才,为画册的最终问世提供了巨大的帮助。在此深表感谢!

最后,感谢所有在此次艺术收藏活动和画册出版过程中给予我们帮助的人士,没有他们的关心和支持,本画册将难以付梓。让我们共同将中国版画艺术介绍给世界,让世界更了解中国!

马 蕾

2006年4月1日

马蕾

Lucy Ma

Postscript

Over the last year, on behalf of the Managing Directors of Novel Energy Ltd.(Canada), I have been coordinating the project of collecting and exhibiting the works of art acquired by the Company President Pa Wong. From the very first hatching of the project to the final publication of this catalogue it has been more than a year of hard work, finally to see success, to hold the catalogue in one's hand, with a happy heart.

Following the initiative of the Company President Pa Wong, the project of collecting the works of art has received assistance and support from Qi Fengge, Dean of the Department of Fine Art in Shenzhen University and from the sixteen famous printmakers included in the catalogue; in the course of my contact with the Chinese printmakers my profound impression of them was their happiness, strong desire and willingness to introduce the arts of Chinese printmaking to the world. Now, I also fervently hope that this project will help them achieve this fine aim.

A year has passed, thanks to the organization of the three teachers Qi Fengge, Qijia Dawa and Zhong Xi, the catalogue's editorial committee met on five occasions in Shenzhen University to jointly consider the catalogue's layout and printing, doing all they could to take the best works to present to the field of Chinese printmaking and to those friends with a love of the art of Chinese printmaking worldwide.

During the same period an old friend in the field of Chinese printmaking, retired professor David Barker, was undertaking the task of translating this catalogue into English, moreover in December 2005 he came in person to Shenzhen University to join the regularly convened editorial committee to contribute valuable advice regarding improvements to the catalogue. At this point, I should like to extend sincere thanks to this international friend for his deeply held regard for the art of Chinese printmaking.

During the process of creating this catalogue, the very able teacher of photography Jin Tielu undertook the work of providing photography for the catalogue, making specialized photographs of each print, giving no little added beauty to the catalogue, sincere thanks are due to Jin Tielu for the help he provided.

Mr. Wong especially appointed Liu Shuang of the Fine Art College of Shanghai University to take an active part in this project, assisting both the artists and the catalogue by taking photographs, for this we express sincere thanks.

During the process of publishing this catalogue, the Artron Inc., one of the most famous companies gave us so many helps. When Mr. Wan Jie, the President of Artron, knew our efforts in promoting Chinese culture, he chose some excellent employees to help us in editing and publishing, we herewith express our sincere thanks.

Finally, thanks are due to all the persons who have been helpful in the collecting of the works and in the publication of the catalogue, without their concern and support this catalogue would have proved difficult to bring to press. Kindly allow us to jointly introduce Chinese printmaking arts to the world, allowing the world to understand China better.

Lucy Ma

April. 1. 2006

图书在版编目（CIP）数据

爱我中华：中国现代版画藏品集／齐凤阁编著 .－北京：中国华侨出版社，2006.5
ISBN 7-80222-113-7

Ⅰ．爱... Ⅱ．齐... Ⅲ．版画－作品集－中国－现代 Ⅳ．J227

中国版本图书馆 CIP 数据核字 (2006) 第 038397 号

爱我中华
中国现代版画藏品集

出　版　社	中国华侨出版社
责任编辑	王　晖
封面设计	钟　曦
装帧设计	王慧英　郑华批　李炜平
篆　　刻	王正光
英文翻译	大卫巴克
图版摄影	金铁路
人物摄影	刘　双

印　　制	北京雅昌彩色印刷有限公司
开　　本	235mm × 305mm
印　　张	20
印　　数	5,000
书　　号	ISBN 7-80222-113-7/J · 1
定　　价	268.00 元

For the love of China
A Collection of contemporary Chinese Prints

Publishing House	The Chinese OverseasPublishing House
Duty Editor	Wang Hui
Cover Designer	Zhong Xi
Layout Designer	Wang Huiying Zheng Huapi Li Weiping
Seal Cuffer	Wang Zhengguang
Translator	David Barker
Photographer of prints	Jin Tielu
Photographer of people	Liu Shuang

Printing	Beijing Artron Colour Rrinting Co.,Ltd.
Page size	235mm×305mm
Printed sheet	20
Printing Copies	5,000
ISBN	7-80222-113-7/J·1
Price	RMB 268.00